CHASSIS & SUSPENSION
HANDBOOK

How to Build Rugged Off-Road Suspensions For Chevy, Ford, Jeep and Dodge Vehicles

From the Editors of *4-Wheel & Off-Road* Magazine

HPBOOKS

HPBooks
are published by
The Berkley Publishing Group
A division of Penguin Putnam Inc.
375 Hudson Street
New York, New York 10014

First edition: February 2003

ISBN: 1-55788-406-4
© 2003 Primedia, Inc.
10 9 8 7 6 5 4 3 2 1

This book has been catalogued with the Library of Congress

Book design and production by Michael Lutfy
Cover design by Bird Studios
Cover photos by *4-Wheel & Off-Road* magazine
Interior photos by author unless otherwise noted

CONTENTS

ACKNOWLEDGMENTS

Although this publication is a team effort between Primedia and HPBooks, it is made possible by the individual efforts of Craig Nickerson, president of Primedia, Inc.; Dave Cohen, vice president of Sales and Marketing;Rick Péwé, Editor of *4-Wheel & Off-Road* magazine; Sean Holzman, Martha Guillen and Eric Goldman, Primedia Licensing. The following writers, editors and photographers also need to be acknowledged for their contributions: John Cappa, Wendy Frazier,David Freiburger, Christian Hazel, Alan Huber, David Kennedy, Craig Perronne, Rick Péwé, and Cole Quinnell.

Building a 4x4 from scratch or modifying your existing rig is extremely popular these days, whether you have a basic bare bones budget project or a mega-buck job. Whichever way you've chosen to build your rig, having some reference material is a big help. The question has always been where can I get the right information, and we're here to help you with just that. From big truck lifts to converting your two-wheel drive to a 4x4, the information you need is now in your hands in one single volume.

4-Wheel & Off-Road magazine has been around for over a quarter of a century, and through the years it has developed into the premier source for real world wheeling information. To this end, we've selected a series of technical articles to help you modify your own 4x4. Some of these stories have been requested many times in reprint form, and now we have collected those and other timely works into one reference, the *Chassis & Suspension Handbook*.

Even though one book is never enough to answer all of your questions, we hope that this volume will help you in your quest to improve your off-road experience. The information in this book represents the best efforts of the editors and contributors of our magzine. Our future plans call for more volumes in this series, covering axles, gearing, engines, and other off-road modifications suited to any off-road vehicle, from mild to all-out. From hard-core buildups or to off-roading basics, we've tried to offer something for everyone in this book, which has always been the guiding philosophy of *4-Wheel & Off-Road* magazine.

Rick Péwé, Editor, *4-Wheel & Off-Road* magazine

All About Spring Rates

By Alan Huber
Photography by Alan Huber and 4WOR Archives

The next time you're shopping for a suspension lift kit, do yourself a favor and don't buy whatever your friends are running on their trucks. At least not before doing a little research (and perhaps soul-searching) on your own to decide how you'll be using your vehicle. Nowadays, even simple, solid-axle kits can cost hundreds of dollars—and that's without any optional kit equipment, shocks, or the new taller tires you'll want to install.

Along with proper steering and suspension geometry, spring rate is one of the most important design aspects of any lift kit. Although spring rate can be defined simply as the amount of weight necessary to compress a spring 1 inch, matching the correct rate to a specific vehicle and its usage is as much art and opinion as it is science and engineering.

Jumping, tough-truck racing, and mud bogging all require stiffer springs than the flexible twist wanted for high ramp-travel indexes and rockcrawling. If you use your 4x4 for these activities and day-to-day pavement pounding, a spring-rate compromise will be needed. This may involve trial-and-error, experience, a good discussion with a techline operator, and a fair assessment of your personal driving needs.

What Are the Rates?

There are other types of rates related to suspension design as well. Wheel rate is how much force the spring and suspension places on the tire contact patch. Due to the fact that the springs mount inboard from the wheel and tire, the lever-arm effects of the axle (or control arms on independent suspensions) make this number less than the spring's rate.

Load rate (or load-carrying capacity) tells us how much weight the spring can carry. Too much weight on a spring with a low-load rate can

quickly sag or even break the springs in extreme cases.

Roll rate measures the suspension's resistance to body roll (body lean) while cornering. Figuring roll rate requires knowledge of a vehicle's center-of-gravity, roll axis, motion ratio, and other data, and the mathematics to put all these figures together. Suffice it to say that factory and aftermarket engineers are extremely careful with roll rates because a truck with too high a center of gravity and too-soft springs can be unstable or downright dangerous to drive during medium- to high-speed maneuvers.

A spring's softness or firmness is its static spring rate and is usually measured with the spring off the vehicle. This spring rate is what we'll be discussing here.

Seasonal Rates

Static spring rates come in two varieties: constant (also called fixed or linear) and variable (also called progressive or non-linear). A constant rate spring takes the same amount of weight to compress each inch of spring travel. In other words, if a spring takes 250 pounds to compress the first inch, theoretically it will

1

Leaf-spring rates can be easily determined using one of the following methods. Intercomp Company has a spring-rate test fixture that uses a hydraulic jack to compress the spring and a force scale to determine the rate. The low-buck (albeit less-accurate) alternative is to have a friend stand on the leaf pack and measure the difference in the spring deflection (compressed arch height versus the relaxed height or free arch). The heavier your friend is, the more accurate your results will be. Divide your friend's weight by the amount of deflection you measured. You can convert your findings to pounds per-inch.

width, and number of leaves. Leaf-end design can also affect spring rate, and most modern designs use friction-reducing items such as tapered ends and pads made of polytetraflour-oethylene (Teflon).

Coil springs can be either constant- or variable rate, depending on whether their coils are wound an equal distance apart (constant-rate) or vary from tightly to loosely wound (variable-rate). Spring rate is changed by metallurgy, wire diameter (thicker wire gives a higher rate) and the distance between each coil (pitch), with tighter windings reducing spring rate.

Torsion bars are almost always constant-rate, with the twisting action of the bar providing spring rate. The bar's rate can be made higher (stiffer) by metallurgy, by increasing the bar's diameter, or by decreasing its length. The real benefit of torsion bars is that you can easily change their load rate by cranking in preload (by tightening their lever-adjusting bolts). This unique feature allows a vehicle to accommodate extra weight such as a winch or a big-block swap. A higher preload can return the truck to its original ride height but also increases the effective spring rate.

What Do I Rate?

Going back to our opening paragraph, how do you choose a suspension kit with the proper spring rate for your vehicle and the type of driving you'll be doing? The most important thing to remember is that there is no perfect-for-all-occasion spring rate. A certain rate might ride great under a heavy, fully optioned, big-block–equipped fullsize truck, but if that same rate spring is installed in a lightweight, stripped-down 4x4, it

require an additional 250 pounds for each additional inch of compression. A variable-rate spring may take 150 pounds to deflect the first inch, 200 pounds for the second inch, 250 pounds for the next inch, and so on.

How Do They Rate?

The three main designs used in today's 4x4s are coil, multiple-leaf,

and torsion bar. The spring rate for each is achieved differently. Leaf springs, comprised of packs of progressively shorter leaves, are considered variable-rate because the longer leaves deflect more easily than the shorter leaves. This means the spring becomes progressively firmer as it compresses. Spring rate is affected by leaf metallurgy, thickness,

will be overly stiff.

If you're into rockcrawling and axle articulation, a low spring rate will give more axle droop and compression, keeping the tires in better contact with the ground. The drawback to this axle action appears on the paved road home, as the soft springs allow high levels of body roll in the corners. If this body roll is excessive, some sort of anti-sway bar (but with disconnects for the trail) will be necessary for safety's sake.

Trailer-towing rigs and many mud racers need the axle control of higher spring rates. Stiff springs reduce axle wrapup under heavy acceleration forces, and their higher load rates help keep heavy trailers stable at speed. As you can see, knowing your truck and your driving style is much more important than any spring's rate spec.

Call the suspension manufacturers listed in the source box and discuss your particulars with their tech departments. Several companies have two lines of springs (heavy-duty or softer-rated). And each company engineers its springs to work in specific kits for specific vehicles at specific heights so that roll rates will stay in the safe zone. Mixing springs from different makers can cause undesirable results, so let the tech departments help you make an informed choice.

Choose a kit based on an honest assessment of your truck and the driving you'll be doing—not what your friends say or what's popular on the trail. Show you care and don't become another lifted truck statistic for the tabloid news-show producers.

If you want to reduce the spring rate of your leaf-pack (or at least limber it up a little), take the pack apart and polish each leaf, grind the ends and tips to round off sharp edges, repaint (some people even wax each leaf), add Teflon liners between the leaves, and reassemble with bolt-type clamps or loosely crimped cinch clamps. There aren't many things that can be done to help coils or torsion bars to flex more.

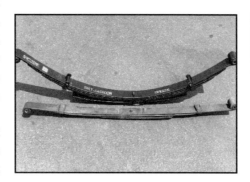
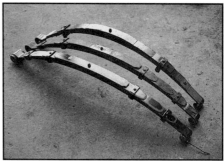

Some interesting dichotomies spring up when comparing leaf springs with different arches. All other things being equal, if a leaf spring is reformed for more arch, the spring becomes stiffer as its arch increases. Because new leaf springs with high arches are also given more length to place the shackles at the proper angles, they are sometimes softer than the lower-arched springs. Flat leaf springs are considered more desirable than high-arch ones for suspension flex because they let the axles droop equally as well as they compress. You can see in the photo that the high-arch spring will not allow much droop, but the high arch gives you the lift and clearance you want for larger tires and larger rocks.

A leaf spring in action! Note that the main leaf flexes more than the shorter ones and also before the others. These leaves show a tapered-end design with attached friction-reducing pads. The bottom leaf is for overload conditions and so is not tapered since its use is infrequent (only with heavy loads). The bolt has been removed from the spring clamp, which nets an extra smidgen of flex from the pack since the main leaf is now free to bend past the bolt hole.

When deciding on a suspension kit, let the manufacturer know if you have any non-stock, weight-increasing equipment on your truck. Winches with their bumpers and mounts can add 100 to 200 pounds or more. If you've swapped in a big-block or added a snowplow, the extra weight can cause soft springs to sag enough to negate the lift you wanted, upset your steering geometry, or even let your tires contact (read: damage) your fenders.

Coil springs have the benefit of being produced with either constant- or variable-rate designs (top and bottom, respectively). Coils also have no internal friction, unlike the leaves of a leaf spring. Nor do they need to position the axle: They simply provide spring rate, leaving positioning chores to trailing (or leading) arms and track bars. Note how the coils of the spring in the second photo are wound progressively looser from top to bottom, creating a variable-rate spring.

Stone-stock factory springs can be surprisingly supple. Especially if they're decades old and have lost most, if not all, of their temper. They are not, however, confidence-inspiring under heavy braking or hard cornering. Suspension manufacturers can produce flexible springs as well, but, since their springs usually also provide lift, they must have a higher rate than stock to compensate for the higher vehicle center-of-gravity, thereby keeping the roll rate under safe control.

Rate Chart

There are some things you should know about this chart. A couple of manufacturers were reluctant to provide spring rate information for publication. The reason for this is that, surprisingly, there is no standard way of measuring spring rate. It can be measured over the first inch of travel or the last inch. It can be measured at installed ride height or...not. Superlift told us it measures rate at installed ride height and 2 inches above and below and takes an average of the three. Skyjacker reports that spring rate can vary by as much as plus-or-minus 3 percent. So which value is correct? The highest or the lowest figure can be published for marketing purposes and not be considered wrong. So don't live by spec charts alone. We've tried to show a few of the most popular solid-axle applications—4-inch lifts for fullsizes and 2 1/2-inch lifts for Jeep CJs. Any more would not have fit our limited number of pages. If your vehicle isn't listed, call the companies named in the source box at the end of this book.

Select Available Rates (All are 4-inch lifts and front springs except where noted. Jeep is either 2 1/2- or 3-inch.)

Make and Model	Suspension Manufacturer	Spring Rate (lbs/in)	Number of Leaves (or coil wire diameter in inches)	Free Arch (or free length for coils) in inches
'73–'87 Chevrolet 1/2-ton pickup				
	Pro Comp (11411)	520	5	3.72
	Rancho Suspension (RS86206)	520	5	3.72
	Rough Country (8002)	604	5	3.48
	Skyjacker (C140S)	490	5	5.00
	Superlift "H.D." (01-234)	605	6	4.125
	Superlift "Superide" (01-234-6)	560	5	4.375
	Tuff Country "H.D." (TCI-C4HD)	395	4	4.75
	Tuff Country "EZ-Ride" (TCI-C4M)	295	3	5.75
	Warn "standard" (721013)	672	5	4.75
	Warn "E-Z Ride" (721014)	490	2	5.00
'74 1/2–'93 Dodge 1/2-ton pickup				
	Pro Comp	N/A	N/A	N/A
	Rancho Suspension (RS420545)	605	5	3.19
	Rough Country (8003)	499	6	4.02
	Skyjacker (D400S)	500	5	4.75
	Superlift, 5-inch "H.D." (01-444)	N/A	5	5.50
	Superlift 5-inch "Superide" (01-444-6)	N/A	5	5.50
	Tuff Country (TCI-D4M)	345	3	5.25
	Warn (723013)	625	5	4.75
'73–'79 Ford 1/2-ton pickup				
	Pro Comp, for '80-'96 models (24412)	520	0.807	18.50
	Rancho Suspension, 3-inch (RS601)	545	0.781	18.68
	Rough Country (9260)	580	0.812	20.00
	Skyjacker (174)	516	0.781	18.875
	Superlift (114)	N/A	N/A	N/A
	Tuff Country (FX4-CL)	450	0.813	19.75
	Warn (702403)	396	0.750	19.50
'76–'86 Jeep CJ5, -6, -7, and -8				
	Pro Comp (front, 51212)	325	5	5.50
	Pro Comp (rear, 51222)	290	5	5.60
	Rancho Suspension (front, RS44092)	325	5	5.50
	Rancho Suspension (rear, RS44192)	290	5	5.60
	Rough Country (front, 8007)	397	6	5.00
	Rough Country (rear, 8008)	281	5	5.33
	Skyjacker (front, J20FS)	240	5	6.00
	Skyjacker (rear, J20RS)	220	5	6.625
	Superlift, "H.D." (front, 01-530F)	330	4	5.75
	Superlift "H.D." (rear, 01-530R)	403	3	5.75
	Superlift "Superide" (front, 01-530F-6)	330	4	5.75
	Superlift "Superide" (rear, 01-530R-6)	380	3	6.00
	Tuff Country "H.D." (front, TCI-J2FM)	405	4	6.25
	Tuff Country "H.D." (rear, TCI-J2RM)	405	4	6.25
	Tuff Country "EZ-Ride" (front, TCI-J2FEZ)	190	5	6.75
	Tuff Country "EZ-Ride" (rear, TCI-J2REZ)	200	5	6.75
	Warn (front, 781131)	267	5	6.75
	Warn (rear, 781132)	244	5	6.562

Spring-Over vs. Stock

Is It Worth It?

By David Freiburger
Photography by Ed Fortson and David Freiburger

The nearly original flatfender was surprisingly capable despite its rock-hard, thick, aftermarket leaf springs. Even so, the spring-over conversion managed to flex the springs more than the stock configuration.

After years of witnessing on-trail action, we have some pretty good ideas about the pros and cons of spring-over versus spring-under axle suspension for lifting your trail vehicle. We don't know it all, though, and are always eager to learn more. So we decided to conduct a few tests to bring both you and us that much closer to wisdom. In Chapter 32, you can read about how we took two similar CJ-7s and treated one to a spring-under lift and the other to a spring-over lift, both of the same height. In doing this, we learned the technical glitches involved with both as well as the real-world, tires-on-the-trail reality of what works best. But for now, here's more of a theoretical look at how converting from stock to spring-over can affect the dynamics of flex.

The Test

We began with a '47 Willys CJ-2A that was mechanically stock with the exception of a 225 V-6, ancient 2 1/2-inch-lift springs, and Mickey Thompson 31x10.50-15 Baja Radial MTX treads. To check the flex of each suspension configuration, we used Tri-County Gear's forklift to lift one tire as far as possible before any other tire lifted off the ground. Sort of like a ramp-travel test without the ramp. We lifted the right front tire first, then moved to the right rear. With the suspension maxed out, we measured the total height of the tire at the inside of the tread, then used a digital angle finder to check the slope of the axles and several points on the frame. The angle measurements gave us an idea of what portions of the Jeep were doing the flexing.

Spring-Under Suspension

We removed the shocks so they wouldn't be a limiting factor, then lifted away. The chart reveals the measurements we found, none of which were particularly surprising. We noted that when lifting the right front tire, the first tire to come off the ground was the right rear; when lifting the right rear, the first tire to lift was the left rear. This isn't too uncommon, since the weight of the engine tends to keep the front end planted, but this could also indicate that the rear suspension has less droop than the front.

Spring-Over Suspension

We converted the flatfender to spring-over using the same springs, axles, and wheels and tires. We gained exactly 1 1/2 inches of tire lift height at both the front and the rear with this one simple change. At both front and rear, the axles gained about 2 degrees of articulation on the angle finder. Comparing the slopes of the front and rear bumpers revealed that the Jeep's frame had another degree of twist, and the body itself leaned over an extra 1.5 degrees.

Based on this, it seems that the

spring-over configuration was able to provide added articulation for two reasons. First, the spring-over seems to put more leverage on the springs—perhaps because the main leaf is farther from the axleshaft centerline—thereby making them work more and allowing the axle to move to a more extreme angle. Second, the lift raises the roll center of the Jeep, which means the entire weight of the body can put more load on the suspension as it flexes. When comparing a spring-over lift to a spring-under setup of the same height, this wouldn't be a noticeable benefit. The increased height also contributed to increased body roll, and we've noticed that this is a problem with spring-over lifts even when compared to spring-under lifts of the same height.

Big Meats

Part of the reason you lift your 4x4 is to fit large tires, so we added a set of 36x13.50-15 Mickey Thompson Baja Kings on 15x10s to see how they would affect things with the spring-over. The true height of the smaller tires was 29 1/2 inches, and the Baja Kings measured 35 inches tall, thereby lifting the Jeep another 2 3/4 inches. In theory, we should have been able to lift each tire 2 3/4 inches more than before, because even if the springs flexed the exact same amount, the tire opposite the one being lifted is starting at 2 3/4 inches higher than it was with the small tires. In fact, we only picked up 1 3/4 inches up front and 2 1/2 in the rear. That's about right for the rear, give or take some tire flex. But why the loss up front?

When you lift a tire with a ramp or a forklift, you mostly work the suspension at the opposite corner of

How High Will a Spring-Over Lift It?

In the example of the flatfender shown in this chapter, swapping the same springs from the bottom of the axles to the top lifted the body 6 inches. But how could we have predicted that number? You can approximate the amount of lift a spring-over will give you by adding up the diameter of the axletube, the height of the weld-on spring perch, and the thickness of the spring pack. All that stuff acts just like a lift block when you relocate the springs. Our Jeep had 3-inch axletubes plus 3/4-inch perches and 2 1/4-inch-thick spring packs. Add it up and you get 6 inches.

Flex Test Results

	Stock	Spring-Over	Spring-Over W/Big Tires
Front tire lift height (in)	19 3/4	21 1/4	23
Front axle slope (deg.)	20.6	22.4	23
Front bumper slope (deg.)	14.2	16.6	16.6
T-case crossmember slope (deg.)	12.7	14.2	13.8
Rear bumper slope (degrees)	10.4	11.7	11.1
Rear tire lift height (in)	18	19 1/2	22
Rear axle slope (degrees)	18.7	20.7	23.3
Front bumper slope (degrees)	6.4	7.9	9.1
T-case crossmember slope (deg.)	9.6	11.2	13.3
Rear bumper slope (degrees)	11.4	13.8	15.7

the vehicle because that's where the weight is being transferred. As we lifted the right front, the too-big Baja King stuffed itself into the sheetmetal of the wheelwell at the right rear, putting an end to compression travel. That caused the left rear to unload sooner than before, and prevented us from lifting the front end any farther. Sort of gives you an idea how bumpstops can affect the performance of the entire vehicle, huh? In theory, the bigger, heavier tires should help keep the tread on the ground, but that didn't happen here.

While our flex test makes spring-over suspension seem like the right thing to do from an articulation point of view, there are many drawbacks to consider. As this photo reveals, the angle from the drag link to the tie rod will be totally unacceptable if you use the stock components. One solution is the trick new spring-over steering setup from Tri County Gear, which relocates the tie rod above the leaf springs to move it out of boulders' reach while also helping to prevent bumpsteer and steering-rod-to-spring interference problems.

When deciding to go to larger tires, here's how you can figure out how much they'll lift the vehicle: Subtract the measured height of the smaller tires from the measured height of the larger tires, and divide by two. In our example, the 31x10.50-15 Baja Radial MTXs were 29 1/2 inches tall, and the 36x13.50-15 Baja Kings were really 35s. Subtract 29 1/2 from 35 and you get 5 1/2 inches; divide by two, and you'll know that the vehicle will be 2 3/4 inches taller.

As a rule, we think a trail vehicle should have at least enough wheel travel to drive over an obstacle that's as high as the tires. We achieved a maximum lift height (one tire raised off the ground without lifting any other tire) of 21 1/2 inches to the inside edge of the tire when running 29 1/2-inch tires. That's not very good. Even in spring-over configuration, this suspension was severely hampered by very stiff, short springs.

Our quick test didn't take advantage of the fact that a spring-over should really be done with leaf springs that are flat or have very little arch. Not only do flat springs move easier, their length doesn't change as much when they arch under compression and extension. As you can see here, the rear tire has moved forward under droop. Actually, the entire rear axle is no longer square in the chassis because the arched leaf springs became much longer under compression on the driver side and much shorter during droop on the passenger side. Therefore, one wheel moved forward and the other pushed rearward. That doesn't happen as much with flat springs.

Droop, Twist, Flex

We Tackle the Shackle

By David Kennedy
Photography by David Kennedy and Verne Simons

Thin strips of steel, bent into an arch, stacked together in one big pack—that's all leaf springs are. They're brutally simple and hardly ever fail, and their beauty lies in the fact that they both locate the axle and spring the vehicle's weight without needing any links, track bars, or coil springs. But it's this simple design that also limits their potential when you head off road.

What if you want to make a leaf spring suspension work better? We mean more than just bolting on a lift kit. We mean adding suspension flex, softening the ride, and increasing axle articulation. You can play with different leaf packs to get exactly the right spring rate and number of leaves, but we decided to experiment with Goodrich's Velvet-Ride, and Teraflex's Revolver shackles to see what effect they would have on our leaf-sprung test vehicles. You can check us out doing our Dukes of Hazard impersonations...er... suspension testing at www.4wheel offroad.com. Yes the truck broke when we landed, but the shackles held up just fine.

Goodrich Velvet Ride Shackles

Teraflex Revolver Shackles

9

Just like you, we broke out the jackstands for the installation work in our driveway. Hey, we're not hydraulic lift snobs—we just wish we were! Save yourself some headaches by removing the rear tires from the truck to make sure the leaf springs can reach full droop. You'll have to remove four factory bolts (two per side) to get the stock shackles out. These bolts are probably held on with a healthy dose of rust or thread lock. Use a torch, breaker bar, or speed wrench (aka hammer) as necessary to remove them.

The Goodrich Velvet-Ride shackles replace the stock shackles with a two-piece hinge design that adds a torsion bar with a soft initial rate to the shackle. The theory is that this softer rate spring in the shackle will compress much easier than your 3/4- or 1-ton leaf springs to take out some of the jarring ride you get driving around in an unloaded pickup. Don't worry, you won't lose any of the weight capacity of your truck with these shackles (but we did lose about 1 1/2 inches at unloaded ride height). When you load down the rear suspension, the Velvet-Ride Shackles bottom out and let the leaf spring still do the heavy work.

How does the truck ride with the new shackles? We'll still suck Larry Ragland's dust on the fast gravel roads even with the new rear shackles, but they do take some kick out of the rear suspension. The most noticeable ride improvement actually showed up on our commute into work. We use to feel every manhole cover, expansion joint, and imperfection in the road more than 1/4 inch tall. A lot of these little bumps are now soaked up by the Velvet-Rides. You should still expect to spill your coffee when crawling over Honda Civics.

Axle hop was never a problem, even with our long rear leaves and 4-inch blocks, and we're happy to report that the new shackles haven't compromised any of that. We do feel a slight unloading of the rear suspension from time to time when we let off the brakes and launch the truck from a stoplight, but it is barely noticeable.

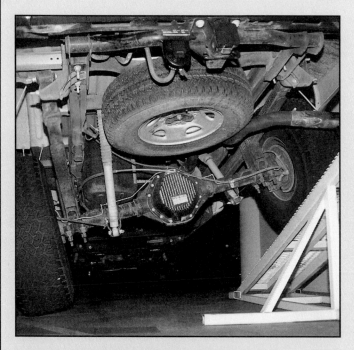

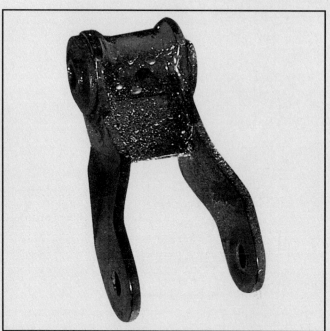

Nobody is suggesting that the Velvet-Ride shackles will improve your suspension's flex, but they won't limit your suspension's travel either. We think it's possible that the softer initial flex of the shackle allows for a little more compression and droop than the stock shackles permit. RTI numbers for our IFS 3⁄4-ton are so low we won't even publish them, but we had to try it.

With it sitting next to the factory shackle off of our Jeep Cherokee, you can clearly see that this is no conventional shackle. The Revolver shackle not only lets the leaf spring travel front to rear as the suspension cycles, but it can also permit twisting and an obscene amount of droop due to its hinge function.

Depending on the year, make, and model of your vehicle you might have to do like we did and hack off the end of the tailpipe for clearance. The Revolver shackles push the leaf springs away from the frame (the rear of our truck now sits an inch taller than stock) and may allow the springs to hit the exhaust as they did on our truck. To install the Revolvers, remove the rear shocks and jack the truck up by the frame to let the rear spring go to full droop. In our case we took the rear tires off because our weenie jack and jackstands were designed for working on cars.

Here's the Revolver shackle when the rear suspension is at full droop. Our Cherokee went from a stock RTI score of 517 to 567 with the Revolver shackles. Remember that the shocks are now the limiting factor in suspension droop, as these shackles can open way up to let the spring move.

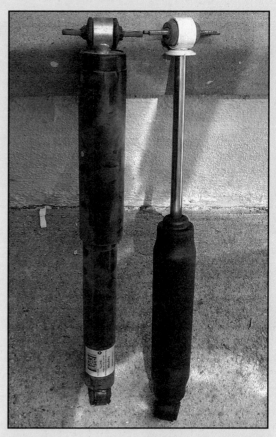

Revolver Applications

Vehicle	Part Numbers	
	Front	**Rear**
CJs '41–'75	RCJ-E	RCJ-E
CJs '76–'86	RCJ-F	RYJ-F
YJs	RYJ-F	RYJ-R
XJs	n/a	RXJ
Samurai	RCJ-F	RCJ-F
Toyota pickups	n/a	RTOY-T
Toyota 4Runner	n/a	RTOY-T
FJ60, FJ70, FJ80	RTOY-T	RTOY-T
FJ40, FJ45	RFJ-40	RFJ-40
Scout 800 Series	RCJ-F	RCJ-F
Scout II	n/a	RCJ-F
Chevy/GMC S-10/S-15	n/a	RCJ-R

You're going to need longer shocks when you add Revolver shackles. We had an old set of Skyjacker shocks from a 3-inch lift kit in the garage that were about 2 inches longer than the stock Jeep shocks, so we bolted them on. To figure out what shocks you should run, remove your current rear shocks and use an RTI ramp, a forklift, or a nearby trail to fully articulate the rear suspension. Measure the distance from shock mount to shock mount on the compressed side of the suspension. That is your "compressed height." Now measure the distance from shock mount to shock mount on the full droop side. That is your "extended height" measurement. Then, armed with these two measurements, call up your favorite shock manufacturer to get the shocks that will work for you. With the new Revolver shackles, your shocks and driveshaft will become the limiting factor in your suspension's droop. You'll want to pay close attention to pinion angles, especially on heavy, high-horsepower vehicles.

Spring Time

Suspension Is Our Favorite Season

By David Kennedy
Photography by David Kennedy

Ever think about wheeling a sheet of plywood off road? Try it. Have your buddy tow a 4x8-foot sheet of plywood behind his 4x4 down the trail. Heck, even a graded dirt road would do, and you'll develop an appreciation for why so many pages of this book are filled with suspension stories. That's because a truck's suspension is in a dead heat with the four-wheel-drive system when it comes to making our vehicles perform off-road. Think about it. Slapping a Dana 44 axle and a transfer case into a Corvette would not make it an off-road hero. Sure it might have four-wheel drive now, but the limited suspension travel will cripple it when you get to the first rough spot. The second half of the equation (dare we say more important half?) is the suspension.

Wheelin' a Sheet of Plywood

You don't even have to carry out this ludicrous experiment to know the torturous experience that it would be.

Stone-age simple. The leaf spring was around long before four-wheel drive, and their ability to both spring the vehicle and locate an axle makes them a proven piece that kills a whole flock of birds with a single stone.

Coilover shocks depend on coil springs to support the load. In this arrangement, two coils with different rates can be stacked to form a variable rate spring that will feather out the small bumps and still soak up the big air when necessary.

You and the plywood would move together as a single unit and crash and smash over the slightest bumps in the road. You'd be hating life because the lumber you were riding on has no way to absorb the imperfections of the terrain without translating them directly to every square inch of the wood and subsequently your body. You would pitch, dive, and roll with whatever the road had to deal out because the plywood you were riding on has no way to absorb, move, or handle the terrain.

The experience would actually be even scarier because with no suspension, bumps and dips could cause the plywood to come off the ground. Yup, you'd get airborne, and the landings wouldn't be soft ones. Imagine if you had to try and steer, accelerate, and push the brakes on that bad boy—it would never happen! The terminal velocity of your plywood "ride" would be quite low as a result,

topping out somewhere in the neighborhood of 15 mph. Above that and the board would spend more than 75 percent of the time in the air. And that, ladies and gentlemen, is not driving. That kind of experience is more along the lines of what we'd call desert racing.

The Spring Is King

If we wanted to drive vehicles without suspensions we'd all be sled makers or ship builders. Both of these types of vehicles rely on terrain that is almost perfectly smooth. But for those of us who like to travel where the environment is less than perfect, the spring is king. The spring, and we're talking about any spring (coil, leaf, torsion bar, or airbag), permits the wheels and tires of a vehicle to bob and weave, scouting for traction and grip while the rest of the vehicle maintains a much more controlled and even keel. The springs of a vehicle are

a compliant system that soak up the bumps and holes in the earth, sifting out most of the harsh crashing and bashing to let us, the drivers, concentrate on controlling the direction and speed of the vehicle. It is hard to drive when your eyes are watering from the vibration and you're holding on for dear life. To get the proper education on all things springs, we called up Michael Eaton of Eaton Detroit Spring. Michael's company has been manufacturing coil and leaf springs since 1937, and has springs for more than 100,000 applications. So it's safe to say he's a man who knows things about springs.

When designed properly, the springs force the tires into making contact with the terrain while supporting the weight of the vehicle. When choosing springs, your goal should be to maximize suspension travel. For our money, we'd try to err on a spring that was too soft. In other words, a spring with a low "spring rate." If the springs are too stiff, they can become the limiting factor in your suspension travel, and make for a terrible ride. It is important to understand that all springs effect your vehicle's ride height, chassis roll stiffness, pitch resistance, suspension compliance, handling balance, ride quality, and tire adhesion. With all those factors to manage it is no wonder lift kits cost as much as they do.

Variable Rate Springs

In a perfect world your springs would have a variable rate. The best springs would have a soft initial spring rate to absorb the subtle irregularities of the trail, and a much firmer spring rate to handle the larger bumps and jumps and to control sway and axlewrap. It is possible to get this kind of variable rate with both coil and leaf springs. Coil springs use a different coil spacing within the coil spring to effectively change the spring rate. You can tell variable rate coil springs from a traditional progressive rate spring because they have some of their coils tightly packaged together, and the spacing between the coils gets progressively larger. Naturally the longer the spring, the more variable the rate can be.

Leaf springs vary their rates by changing the thickness of the leaves, or by adding "over-load" leaves that may only make contact with the

Spring Lingo

Spring load is the amount of weight it takes to compress the spring to a given height and it is measured in pounds. The spring load determines how much weight the spring can support at a given height. Think weight-carrying capacity.

Spring rate is the amount of force it takes to compress the spring 1-inch and is expressed in lb/in. The spring rate determines how much the spring will compress as the loading increases. Think spring stiffness.

If the front or rear of your truck is sagging you need more spring load, not more spring rate. Spring rate does not change through the life of the spring but spring load will change. Springs sag as a result of the spring steel fatiguing over time and losing their spring load.

Wheel rate is the spring rate actually measured at the wheel (or tire). The wheel rate is usually lower than the true spring rate due to factors such as spring position and control arm or axle leverage that can effectively lessen the spring rate at the wheel versus the actual spring rate at the spring. If you move the spring closer to the tire (and the spring travels parallel to the wheel), the wheel rate and spring rate will become almost the same.

Unsprung weight is the weight of the tires, wheels, knuckles, hubs, solid axles (basically any part of the truck not supported by the springs), and half the weight of the springs, shocks, control arms, and/or links.

Sprung weight is the weight of the body, chassis, drivetrain, tools, parts, and the other half of the total weight of the springs, shocks, control arms, and or links.

chassis when the truck is loaded down. If you look at the rear leaf packs on dualies, you can see how the manufacturers can get massive load-carrying capacities out of these trucks, without compressing your spine when you drive the truck around town with the bed empty.

Coils vs. Leaves

Sorry, but we aren't going to declare a winner in the world of springs because there is no clear cut advantage to either coils or leaves. Coil springs cost less to make, are lighter, have no internal friction, and take up very little space. The downside with coils is that they do not locate the axles. A three- or four-link suspension must be constructed to work with the coil springs to do the

same job that leaf springs alone can do. Leaf springs, on the other hand, are completely modular (if you want to add or subtract lift or load capacity, just add more leaves), do locate the axles, and can also help to reduce sway. The best leaf packs will use multiple thin leaves to provide load control yet still move freely. Yes, leaf springs are heavy, prone to axlewrap, and can require a lot of mounting space. But keep in mind that a suspension's characteristics have more to do with how the whole system is set up (and the spring rates that are used) than it does with whether the springs are leaves or coils. Hey, as low-tech as leaf springs may seem, they can be made to work with maybe just a weight penalty over the coil spring.

Calculating Spring Rates

With all this talk about springs we thought we would give you these two formulas to add to your mental toolbox. We've made it so easy because these formulas will let you calculate spring rates without even removing them from the vehicle.

Leaf Spring Rates

$$\left(\frac{\text{width of leaves (in inches)} \times \text{number of leaves}}{12 \text{ (constant for all leaf springs)}}\right) \times \left(\frac{1000 \times \text{thickness of one leaf (in inches)}}{\text{length of spring (in inches)}}\right)^3 = \text{Leaf Spring Rate}$$

Example: The spring rate for a leaf spring that is 3 inches wide, 52 inches long, has 7 leaves, and each leaf is 0.25-inch thick would work out as follows:

$$\left(\frac{2.25 \times 7}{12}\right) \times \left(\frac{1000 \times 0.25}{52}\right)^3 = 146 \text{ lb/in}$$

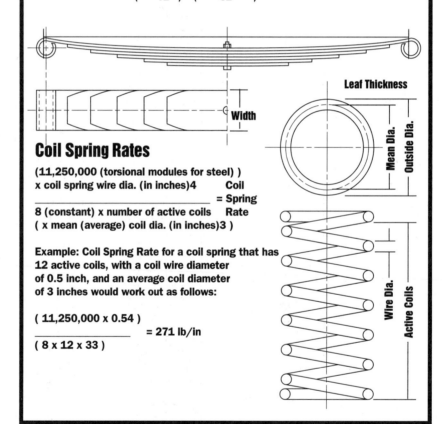

Leaf Thickness
Width
Mean Dia.
Outside Dia.

Coil Spring Rates

$$\frac{(11{,}250{,}000 \text{ (torsional modules for steel)}) \times \text{coil spring wire dia. (in inches)}^4}{8 \text{ (constant)} \times \text{number of active coils} \times \text{mean (average) coil dia. (in inches)}^3} = \text{Coil Spring Rate}$$

Example: Coil Spring Rate for a coil spring that has 12 active coils, with a coil wire diameter of 0.5 inch, and an average coil diameter of 3 inches would work out as follows:

$$\frac{(11{,}250{,}000 \times 0.5^4)}{(8 \times 12 \times 3^3)} = 271 \text{ lb/in}$$

Wire Dia.
Active Coils

Shackle Restoration

5

By David Kennedy
Photography by David Kennedy and Rick Péwé

In the quest for the ultimate utilitarian Jeep, this Flatfender has evolved from years of research and development that has brought it to its current status. Our Editor, Rick Péwé, has been refining it since 1972 and feels he has gotten close to perfection—although he just broke the transfer case adapter, so there are still a few bugs to be worked out.

Knowing that any 4x4 project worth its transfer case is never done, we bring you Flatfender 2001, in which we begin a new chapter in the evolution of a Jeep that will never die. The Darwinian theory of evolution says that only the strong survive, and while some would say that there is not much left to this '45 GPW, we say that there is nothing there that doesn't work!

We began Flatfender 2001 with a suspension restoration of the '45 at T&J's 4-Wheel Drive Automotive Center in Orange, California. This shop knows all things Jeep and is well versed at making them even better. Our cameras could barely keep up with the hands of the technicians at T&J's as they stripped off our old suspension, before sending us down the road to Deaver Spring in Santa Ana.

Deaver Spring was building leaf springs before the Jeep was invented, and handcrafted us a set of its finest leaves based on our Jeep Wrangler packs that were worn beyond recognition. The guys at T&J's reserved a bay for us all day, and stayed late to bolt on our new stuff.

Our tired old Wrangler springs had seen better days. Traction from ARB-locked Boggers had flexed the leaves into right angles, and rear spring wrap was out of control. To remove the worn springs we put the truck on the lift at T&J's so that the leaves relaxed to full droop.

Straps were used to hold the Dana axles to the frame, and impact guns were used to negotiate the release of rusted nuts that the U-bolts were holding hostage.

Strapping the axles to the frame saves you a lot of work. Brake lines as well as shocks can stay attached, and driveshafts need not be removed. Here the front springs are being unbolted from their shackles. Notice the slip-spline of the front driveshaft. Any more droop and the shaft would come apart.

One thing all our rigs have in common is rust. This pesky spring perch had formed a covalent bond with our grade 5 bolt and would not let go. The torch was used to cut the nut off, and the bolt was driven out with a long punch.

Our spring packs had reached their expiration date and were taken to Jeff Crosby at Deaver Spring. Here Crosby points out where one of our front springs had developed a kink in the main leaf. This is the early warning sign of a spring that is about to break.

Crosby used our old springs as a template on which to base our custom-made spring pack. Deaver Springs has been doing this type of work since 1892, and every one of its springs receives the highest level of attention.

Because spring steel has a memory, Deaver selects spring material that has to be de-arched to the desired height. Here the steel is run through a press that essentially flattens the spring. This ensures that your springs will not sag and your desired ride height will be maintained.

Deaver uses its own "snail-wrap" top leaf to reduce axlewrap on all its springs. This top leaf acts like a traction bar, which we hope will keep our pinion angle in check when we dump the clutch on 510 lb-ft of torque. Here you can see the forming of the "snail-wrap" by hand.

Springs are drilled and counter sunk, and spring clamps are riveted into place by hand. The edges of the leaves are ground into a diamond shape to disperse shearing forces that can cause the spring to kink and fail. As an added bonus this custom feature allows the spring to really twist on the trail!

Spring packs used in off-road applications are assembled with thin bronze shims instead of aluminum to reduce friction between leaves.

In this photo you can see the "snail-wrap" formed by the top leaf. This top leaf extends from the leaf pack's centerline forward to control axlewrap without making the spring overly stiff. The pack is bolted together with a center pin, and the spring clamps can be custom fitted to clear your steering components if necessary.

Back at T&J's, the new springs were a routine install. The technicians used a healthy dose of grease and antiseize to make sure everything moved properly.

New Daystar greasable shackles and poly bushings were used front and rear to complete the new suspension system. Springs can be a little tricky to work into position, especially on trail-hardened Jeeps whose frames move just as much as the rest of the suspension.

The new springs were first bolted to the hangers, and then to the axle with new U-bolts made by Deaver. Here a transmission jack is being used to move the Dana 60 into position. This photo simulates the amount of axlewrap we had with the old springs.

The package is completed with a new set of Rancho RS 9000 shocks mounted upside down for clearance reasons. On the other side of the leaf spring is a failed attempt at a traction bar.

We put the Jeep back home in the rocks, and the new springs work great. The ride height is back to where it should be and we get great droop and flex. A real traction bar that works will be our next step.

Built for Slow and Go

By Craig Perronne
Photography by Craig Perronne

6

The interior, like many tube-framed creations, is bare bones. A few gauges, seats, and a shifter keep it simple but functional. Check out the angle of the steering column. A very healthy Chevy 350 puts out 480 hp for going fast, and gobs of torque for climbing rocks. A Holley 750-cfm double pumper carburetor feeds the mill. In the rear of the vehicle is a spare 35-inch Goodyear MT/R, should any of the other four ever fail. Also visible are the 22-gallon RCI fuel cell and spare driveshafts. Up front rests a trussed Dana 44 with an ARB Air Locker and 4.10 gears hiding inside. The axle is attached to the frame with Fox shocks equipped with Eibach coils.

When Randy Ellis of Tempe, Arizona, began to dream of an off-road rig, he envisioned one that could creep over jagged rocks and blast up monstrous dunes with equal prowess. A big motor, flexy suspension, and super-stout running gear were all deemed necessary to blend the world of speed with the slow motion of rockcrawling. The next step was to find a trail rig to use as the foundation for the buildup.

After looking around at plenty of trail rigs and the pros and cons of each, Randy took a major step and decided to hand-fab his own. Managing Rox Off Fabrication in Tempe gave Randy plenty of experience in the art of fabrication, and also allowed him access to all the tools he needed. In the off hours, the tube benders and welder were kept plenty busy making the complete tube frame.

Once the elaborate tube chassis was completed by the team at Rox Off, it was time to stuff it with the best parts. Since the rig was being built for both slow and go, some serious horsepower was desired. Lots of horses (480 to be exact) came in the form of a Chevy 350 equipped with all the goodies. Forcing fuel down the throat of the engine is a Holley 750-cfm carburetor resting on top of a GM Performance manifold. A team of Holley and GM ignition components then ignites the mixture of fuel and air. The spent gases escape from the motor through custom headers built by Rob McCabe.

The transmission is a TH350 automatic prepped by AZ Performance Transmissions of Mesa, Arizona. To continue the stout theme of the drivetrain, the venerable NP205 transfer case was selected to split power to the axles. Speaking of axles, up front rests a fullsize Dana 44 equipped with 4.10 gears and an ARB Air Locker, while the 44's bigger brother, the Dana 60, takes up the rear with an identical locker and gear combo.

Next on tap was to build a flexy suspension for the tube creation. A four-link design was used both front and rear to provide maximum travel.

Fox coilover shocks equipped with Eibach coils were then placed at each corner to smooth out the ride. Goodyear MT/Rs in the 35-inch flavor were mated to MRT wheels to provide traction.

The tubed exoskeleton then needed some skin, so the body of a donor Jeep was cannibalized and grafted into position. The new body was then beautified with a shiny paint job.

Once the exterior was finished, attention was turned to the interior, which was kept simple. Beard seats keep the driver and passenger comfortable, while Auto Meter gauges relay all the critical information needed. With the tuber completed, Randy was successful in building a rig that was fun to drive fast or slow.

Shock Q&A

By David Kennedy
Photography by David Kennedy and John Cappa
Illustrations: King Off-Road Racing Shocks

7

Shock technology in the off-road world is born and bred in desert racing. Everything that is cool, high tech, or effective in the shock marketplace was developed first out on the high desert sands before it hits our trucks. To go along with the shock shootout story and the shock buyer's guide in this book we wanted to bring you some answers to the most common shock questions we get asked.

While researching shocks and suspension designs for an upcoming project vehicle, we spent a lot of time with the King family at their King Off-Road Racing Shocks facility in Garden Grove, California. Their shop uses aerospace technology, backed by the quality you can only find in a family-owned business whose products wear the family name. At the shop we drooled a lot and learned a lot, and we thought we'd share some of the specifics.

Q: What does a shock do?

A: A shock absorber's sole purpose is to control the speed at which the suspension is allowed to move up and down. When a spring (coil, leaf, or torsion bar—it doesn't matter which) is compressed, it stores energy. If you didn't have shocks on your truck it would bounce on its springs like a big rubber ball when this stored energy is quickly released. It's the vehicle's shocks that add the necessary control to the suspension by slowing the speed that the spring energy is released as well as when it's compressed.

Shocks work by changing the energy of

suspension motion into heat. If you don't believe us, take your rig down a rutted dirt road really fast and then get out and feel how hot the shock bodies get. Shocks produce heat from energy through hydraulic friction to resist a spring's natural tendency to bounce. You can think of a shock as a piston that pushes lightweight oil through a valve in the piston face to create a restriction. This type of restriction is called dampening. Shocks can dampen energy both on the compression stroke and the rebound stroke depending on the application, but if they resist the motion of the spring too much, then the tire can lose contact with the ground.

Q: How should I position shocks?

A: In a perfect world shocks would be mounted as close to the wheel as possible, in such a way that they are positioned perpendicular to the direction of suspension travel. If your suspension compresses straight up and down then you want the shocks mounted out by the

ball joint, as close to vertical as possible. This is how Ford mounts the shocks on a Twin Traction Beam front suspension. If you have a leaf-spring front suspension with the shackles in the rear, then it will be to your advantage to mount the shocks slightly raked back, because as the suspension compresses it moves the axle up and to the rear. Leaf-spring GM trucks use this type of mounting on the front suspension. Rear shocks should also be mounted perpendicular to the direction of travel if space allows.

Q: What are the advantages of gas shocks?

A: The shock piston is constantly thrashing up and down to follow the contour of the road as you drive. When this happens, the oil in the shock can be whipped up into a foamy mess like a batch of scrambled eggs. When shock oil gets aerated, it will flow past the valving in the shock in unpredictable ways that can ruin the performance of even the best

dampers.

High-pressure gas shocks are not as susceptible to oil foaming because they use gas pressure (anywhere from 100 to 300 psi of nitrogen) inside the shock body to keep bubbles from forming in the shock oil. The nitrogen gas does not mix with the shock oil, but rather it acts to keep the shock oil molecules packed together, making it harder for air bubbles to form in the first place. Gas shocks have gotten a bad rap as being firmer than regular shocks, but they can be valved to ride just as smoothly as a conventional shock, while still providing consistent dampening that is impossible to match with a regular shock.

Q: What are monotube shocks?

A: A monotube shock such as the Bilstein 5100 series shown in Figure 1 (Edelbrock Performer IAS shocks are also monotubes) uses a single-wall shock tube to encase the piston, shock oil, and pressurized gas. Monotubes are much more precise at dampening than twin tubes because of the higher level of precision they're manufactured to. A single-wall shock will often use a larger-diameter piston and is always more resistant to fade because it can separate the oil from the dead air space and radiate heat much better then a twin-tube shock. Downside? Monotube shocks are not as cheap to build as twin-tube shocks, so the price is always higher.

Q: What are bypass shocks?

A: Bypass shocks are the ultimate in energy dampening—it's as simple as that. Traditional shocks use valving in the head of the shock piston to determine the dampening rates and characteristics of a shock. Bypass shocks do that too, but bypass shocks also use external metering valves that are completely adjustable with a wrench for rebound and compression

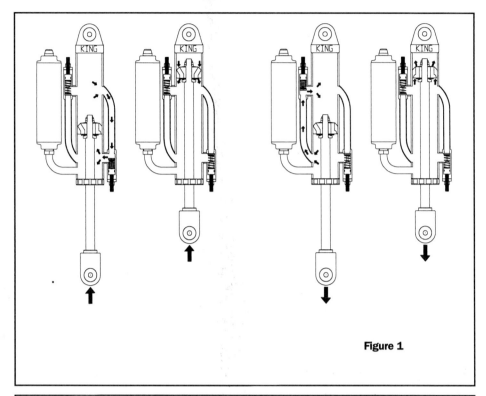

Figure 1

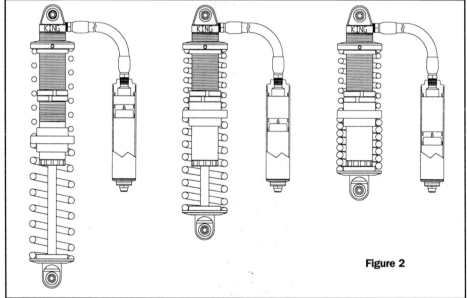

Figure 2

bumps for a smooth ride. Yet they get progressively firmer as the piston compresses farther to the point that they can function as an internal hydraulic bumpstop if the valving in the actual shock piston is set up to do so.

Q: What are reservoir shocks?

A: In Figure 2, you can see a gas pressurized reservoir shock going through its compression cycle. All shocks need some dead air space to allow them to work properly. In a conventional shock that means there must be an air space at the top of the shock or it must use a twin-tube design to allow for expansion. Reservoir shocks also need this dead space, but now the shock body can stay filled with oil at all times because the dead space is in the reservoir, separated from the oil by a floating piston.

The reservoir looks just like a second shock body connected to the shock via a rubber hose or metal tube. Shock oil is transferred back and forth between the shock and the reservoir as the piston in the shock moves up and down. If the air space and the oil are never allowed to mix, the shock will work far better and will provide consistent dampening no matter what the terrain is because there is no aeration.

Q: What type of shock should I run?

A: What kind of shock you should run is really a budget versus application question more than anything. There are a ton of great shocks out there on the market that chassis engineers have spent days in the lab (and on the trail) dialing in to work on your truck. If you're a go-fast driver or like to get air under all four tires, you will really benefit from a reservoir shock's better aeration control and added heat capacity.

dampening. As the shock piston travels upward, compression valving in the shock piston is not the primary source of dampening. Rather, the oil is pushed through the external bypass tube (or tubes) and back under the piston at a rate dictated by the external adjustable check valve. The bypass shock works the same way under rebound dampening, with an external tube(s) that allows shock oil to flow in the opposite direction. Oftentimes

multiple tubes are added for both compression and rebound, and routed to create a shock with almost magical dampening characteristics.

The other secret to the bypass shock's success is that they are position-sensitive and not just velocity-sensitive like conventional shocks. What this means is that bypass shocks can use a valving that is initially light (via the external adjustments) to soak up all the small

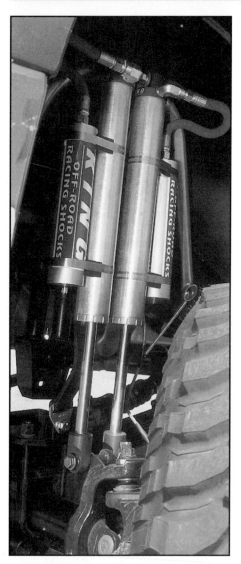

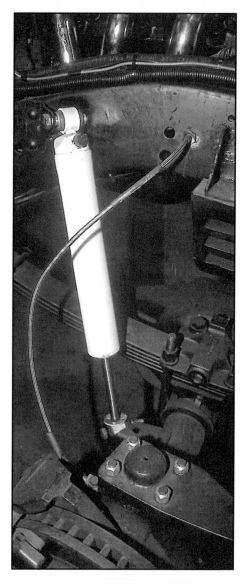

Q: Which is better, rebound or compression dampening?

A: Shocks designed for 4x4s generally use more rebound dampening than compression dampening to smooth out the bumps. By focusing on dampening suspension motion on the rebound, a shock can let the suspension compress easily when a tire hits a bump by letting the spring compress with very little

resistance. This way the spring extension energy is controlled (dampened) by the rebound valving in the shock in a way the driver is much less likely to feel. Good rebound dampening on the rear shocks can help control wheelhop to some degree in the sand and keep the truck from exhibiting excessive brake dive when you perform a panic stop.

A shock still needs a decent amount of compression dampening for the vehicle to handle well. Firm compression valving in the front shocks makes for better turn in and helps keep the nose of the truck level under braking. Firm compression valving in all four shocks will also limit body roll.

Q: Should I run dual shocks?

A: If your truck is experiencing heat-induced shock fade then you could benefit from a dual shock setup so long as the two (or more) shocks are valved properly for your application. When we say "properly" we mean two shocks that are valved lightly to work as a dual shock package. If you just add a second shock with the same valving that the manufacturer called for in a single shock application you will have doubled your dampening. Get ready for a harsh ride! Your suspension could end up being overdampened.

Q: Can I run shocks upside down?

A: As a rule you should not run a dual-tube shock like this RS9000 upside down. Monotube gas shocks such as a Bilstein can be mounted with the shock can up or

down, but most dual-tube shocks will develop an inch or more of "dead space" where an air pocket forms if you mount them improperly. Bottom line: Mount the shocks in the orientation the manufacturer recommends.

The Long Deal

8

By Cole Quinnell
Photography by Cole Quinnell

We all search for the long deal, and in the case of shocks, there are a few advantages to having a longer shaft. Most vehicles come with shocks that are adequate for stock tires and only mild off-roading. They are designed to give the best compromise of on- and off-road performance, fit in the factory location, and be affordable for the OE. If you add larger tires and a lift and want to do more than the occasional blast through the dirt and brush, longer shocks can be beneficial.

Another advantage to the longer shock is the potential for more wheel travel, assuming you select the right one. A longer shock also houses more fluid which means it takes longer to heat up.

Mounting a longer shock can be difficult. Most of the time, you need a custom mount, or an aftermarket dual-shock hoop. In the case of '76–'80 CJ front shocks, the solution is easy. These have the lower mount on the spring plate under the axle. The front is a short tab welded on top of the frame. The '82–'85 CJs used a taller upper shock mount, but the lower mount was on top of the axle tube. By using the '82–'85 upper shock mount with the earlier spring plate lower mount, you can fit a shock approximately 4 inches longer than stock.

That's fine and dandy except that the shock mounts are no longer available from the dealer. We learned that 4 Wheelers Supply now makes them, so we ordered a pair to show you how easy it is to get the long deal.

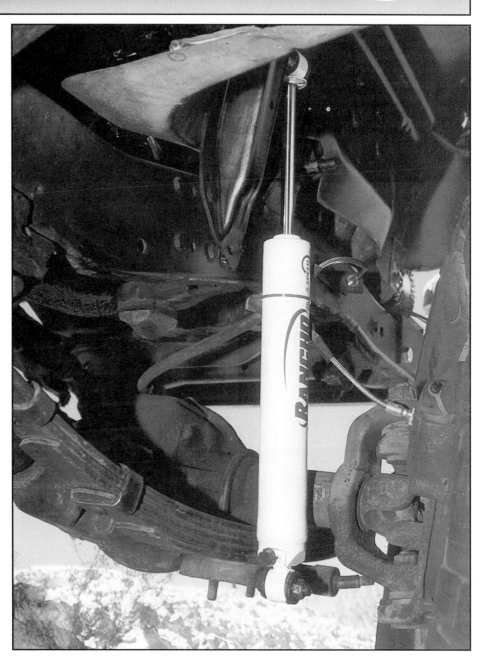

This CJ has a 4-inch Superlift suspension. The Superlift shocks have a total range of 13 1/4 inches compressed to 21 3/4 inches extended. The shocks were bottoming out on the trail (about the same time the 33x12.50s were hitting the fenders) but did not reach full extension. By choosing the correct length shock with the taller upper shock mount, compression shouldn't be limited by the shock any longer.

The new upper shock mounts from 4 Wheelers Supply are very similar to factory mounts used from '82 to '85. We installed the new mounts and shocks in about three hours. We left the old upper mounts in place, but they can be cut off the frame if you prefer. To get started, raise the vehicle and rest the frame on jackstands. Remove the front shocks and tires.

On the driver-side, the fuel return line is in the way. Unbolt the clamp and you can either move the line to the top of the framerail or swing it under the framerail. Either way, drill a new hole and secure the clamp. Check behind the framerails on both sides before drilling holes: It's common for the brake lines to be in the way.

The new shock mounts will be located farther toward the rear of the vehicle than the stock ones. The forward and upper motor-mount bolt lines up with the middle, rear bolt hole on the new shock mount. If you're using the '81-and-earlier lower shock mount, install a socket on the front, lower motor-mount bolt and lean the shock mount on the socket (with the forward, upper motor-mount bolt installed in the shock mount).

Install a shock on the upper mount to check for binding before you drill all the holes or do any welding. After the middle rear bolt is installed, the mounts may need a little grinding to clear the lower front motor-mount bolt.

You can either bolt or weld the mounts to the frame. The disadvantages to bolting them on are that the frame is boxed and it will collapse as you tighten the bolts. The disadvantages to welding are that it's more permanent and not everyone has the needed equipment. If you will be welding on the mount, grind the paint off the frame.

We used the one motor-mount bolt that lines up, drilled one 3⁄8-inch hole, inserted a bolt (but didn't tighten it enough to crush the frame), and welded on the shock mount. The old upper-shock mounts should be cut off, which is much easier with the fenders off the vehicle.

We used a Daytona Mig welder to attach the bottom and one side of the mount to the frame. This will keep the mount from moving at all, which would hog out the holes in the frame where the bolts attach the mount. If you're going to weld, make sure the fuel lines are a safe distance, and be careful of braided steel brake lines.

A little black spray paint makes the new shock mount look nearly original. The new shocks we used are Rancho RS 9000, PN 92126. They measure 13 1⁄2 inches compressed and 26 1⁄2 inches extended and offer adjustability from supersoft to superfirm at the twist of a knob.

Our droop is limited elsewhere, so we didn't gain that with the longer shocks. Although, if your shocks currently limit down travel, then you can improve this with longer shocks. The compression on this Jeep is no longer limited by shock length.

Rancho Shock Comparo

By John Cappa
Photography by Craig Perronne

With all the shocks on the market today, it is difficult to pick what will work best on your four-wheeler. There are several manufacturers, various types of technology, and plenty of hype.

We contacted Rancho to get the three shocks that the company produces. It offers cellular gas shocks (RS 5000), manually adjustable shocks (RS 9000), and the new self-adjusting shocks (RSX). All three of these shocks present distinct advantages.

To test them, we used a '48 flat fender with a very modified spring-over suspension system. You might think that isn't a good example of the typical four-by, and you're right. However, its poor on-road-handling characteristics will give us more defined results than a stock or even a moderately lifted vehicle. It sways horribly in corners—partially due to the lack of sway bars— and dives when braking, and the front lifts under acceleration. It does, however, ride comfortably while going slow as well as fast.

All of this was taken into account when we put each shock through its paces. Since the RS 9000 is actually five shocks in one (five different settings), we tested it on the most extreme settings, 1 and 5. This covers the range of possibilities with the manually adjustable shock.

RS 5000

The RS 5000 is a twin-tube cellular-

For the braking test, we used a smooth, hard-packed dirt road. We accelerated to 30 mph and then locked up the brakes. The compression was measured by a zip tie on the shaft of the shock. We used the same stretch of dirt road for the acceleration test. With the Jeep in two-wheel drive, we started out in second gear. The tires spun a little in most cases, so the amount of lift would probably be increased if measured on pavement. Our rocky section wasn't particularly difficult, but it had enough large rocks to give us an idea how well each shock would absorb the bumps of rockcrawling. The patch was located on a hill, so bumps and jars were accentuated by weight transfer.

The RS 5000.

gas design with 10-stage velocity-sensitive valving. The bushings are made of rubber, and many lengths and mount types are available. Lighter-valved, dual-shock applications are available in 7-, 9-, 11-, and 14-inch travel lengths. The light-valved shocks only come with eye-type mounts.

The RS 5000 rode smooth on the street but swayed some in corners. The ride on rough dirt roads at speed was a little stiff over some of the bigger bumps. The smaller, close-together bumps (washboard) made the vehicle feel like it was hovering above the bumps, and it floated a little from side to side. The rebound was a little quick, which could be attributed to the floating sensation. In the rocky section, the quick rebound was noticeable, but the ride was acceptable. For our braking test, the front RS 5000s squatted 3 inches. (Jump to the captions to see how we tested

brake dive and acceleration lift.) The rebound from the compression was quick but did not cause the vehicle to bob excessively. Under acceleration, the front only lifted 1 inch. If you are on a tight budget and can't afford the more advanced shocks, this is an excellent upgrade from spongy-soft, stock shocks. They would also work well for lifted trucks, since just about any length and mount type is available.

RS 9000

The RS 9000 is a five-position manually adjustable shock. The adjuster changes both compression and rebound damping. It is a tri-tube, cellular-gas design and has 15-stage valving. The bushings are made of red urethane, and many mount types and shock lengths are available. Light-valved versions are available in the same lengths mentioned for the RS 5000.

We tested the RS 9000 first at the No. 1 setting. It provided a smooth ride on the street but swayed quite a bit when we drove quickly through the corners. This is the price you pay for a Cadillac ride. Over the rough dirt road, the shocks rode well. However, big bumps would cause the suspension to bottom out. This was expected with the light valving at No. 1. In the slow rocky section, the shocks rode very well. Damping and rebound seemed spot-on for rock crawling. The front shocks compressed 2 1/4 inches on the braking test and lifted 1 1/4 inches in the acceleration run.

We then tested the RS 9000s at the No. 5 setting. On the street, the shocks rode very stiff. Even the smallest bumps could be felt, and there was almost no sway in the corners. The turn of a knob had turned our wiggle wagon into a pavement carver. We had to slow down for the bigger bumps over the dirt road because it was so stiff. Rockcrawling with the

The RS 9000.

shocks on No. 5 was a nightmare. The stiff valving wouldn't allow the suspension to move. Under the braking test, the front shocks compressed 2 1/4 inches. After we had stopped, we noticed the front end slowly rising back to static height. The front only lifted 3/4 inch under acceleration.

Something to consider with the RS 9000s is that they really are five shocks in one. The five settings offer plenty of adjustability depending on how you want the vehicle to ride. The No. 5 setting was too stiff for our lightweight application, but heavy trucks and loaded-down vehicles need this kind of damping. The cool part about it is that the shocks can be readjusted to get a smooth ride once the truck is empty again. Also, the shocks can be adjusted differently from front to rear to get a smooth ride. These shocks would work well on all types of vehicles, from Samurais to one-tons. Since they can be adjusted, they will work well in a variety of terrain as well as for street use and towing.

RSX

The RSX is a twin-tube, nitrogen gas–charged shock that has Reflex Technology valving. This is what gives the shock its brains. Under normal conditions, the valve is closed. When a harsh bump is encountered, the valve opens, allowing increased oil flow and a smoother ride. This design enables the shock to be valved for greater control without ride quality suffering. The bushings are made from a reinforced silica compound (RSC) that is said to provide twice the durability of standard shock bushings. The RSX shocks are only available in vehicle-specific lengths, mounts, and valving. This meant we had to do some modifications to make them fit our flatfender.

Hardware

The RS 5000s and RS 9000s have a universal valving. One model (5112 and 9112 in our case) will fit many applications. For this reason, lots of hardware is included with most of the shocks. Not all of it will be used. As we stated before, the RSX shocks are built for specific applications. They come with little or no hardware because the mounts on the shocks are custom-fit. In order to fit RSX shocks on this Jeep, we had to search the specifications in the catalog to get the right length and mounts. Even so, we still had to swap bushings around to get them to fit. We ended up with Ford F-250 front shocks on the front and Ranger rear

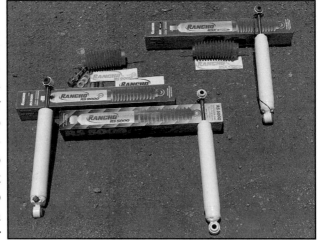

shocks on the rear. Since this Jeep has a V-8, we figured it would test better this way. Applications are available in both stock and lifted versions. Does that mean you can't have RSX shocks if your vehicle isn't listed in the catalog? Certainly not, but expect to do a little bit of research to find the proper length and mounts. Be prepared to change bushings if they won't fit the mounts on your vehicle. It is also a good idea to choose an RSX shock that is for a vehicle with a similar weight and suspension system.

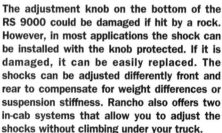

The adjustment knob on the bottom of the RS 9000 could be damaged if hit by a rock. However, in most applications the shock can be installed with the knob protected. If it is damaged, it can be easily replaced. The shocks can be adjusted differently front and rear to compensate for weight differences or suspension stiffness. Rancho also offers two in-cab systems that allow you to adjust the shocks without climbing under your truck.

The RSXs rode a little firm on the street. This is probably because the front shocks we used were designed for the front of an F-250. The rear shocks were for the rear of a Ranger, and they seemed to ride well on the street. It is important to realize that the RSX shocks are designed and valved for specific vehicles. We had to swap

The RSX.

and modify bushings to get them to fit our Jeep. Even so, the ride was acceptable, and we felt only a little sway in the corners. They rode exceptionally smooth at high speeds in the dirt, especially over the larger bumps. We suspect that this is because of the Reflex valving. The RSXs also excelled in the slow, rocky section. We thought they would ride stiff because they rode firm on the street, but the special valve helped absorb the bumps and jerks. They compressed 2 1/2 inches in the braking test and lifted 1 inch under acceleration. The Reflex valving of the

Just for comparison, we tested the Jeep without shocks. At slow speeds the vehicle rode exceptionally well, but once out of first gear low-range it kicked and bucked like a mad bull. The excessive bouncing caused the driveshafts to bind several times, making a noise we hope never to hear again. We did, however, gain travel with the shocks removed. The shocks had been the limiting factor, so the tires now wadded up into the fenders and drooped a little further. Would we recommend not running shocks? Not a chance.

RSX is the reason for its success. For anyone not wanting to mess around with knobs, the RSX is the way to go. The firmly valved shocks will work well on many types of vehicles and terrain, although the applications are somewhat limited.

Building a Better Transfer Caseless

By John Cappa
Photography by John Cappa and Scott Killeen

10

We can hear it now: "Can't you guys even read the name of your magazine? Why did you put two-wheel drives bla bla bla?" Sure, we can read. All trucks have four tires and can be driven off-road, right?

Let's face it, some of the fastest, best handling off-road trucks are two-wheel drives. These are the desert race trucks of SCORE and the closed-course trucks of CORR. Most of us can't afford these $100,000-plus vehicles that belong in Fortune and other you'll-never-own-this magazines. That's not what you'll find here. What you will find is the different kinds of lifts for two-bys and the design and function of each.

The Premise

While a two-by will never compete with the traction that a four-wheel drive offers, it can have its advantages. Less drivetrain maintenance, cheaper initial cost, and cheaper insurance, plus the fact that many 4x4s are destined to never have the transfer case engaged and serve only as street transportation, are all valid reasons for owning a two-by. Two-bys also make great tough truck competitors—why destroy a perfectly good 4x4?

Now, you can ruin your two-by and turn it into a belly-dragging barrio cruiser that gets hung up on speed bumps with groceries in the bed, or you can do the right thing and try to get a little performance and lift out of

the suspension. We would rather see the lifted versions. Not all 4x4s hit the dirt, and the same can be said of lifted two-bys. Many are built just for the look of a 4x4. And while we don't condone this activity, it's still better than owning a lowered truck or souped-up import car.

IFS Sucks, Normally

Independent front suspension isn't all that bad. However, adding a drive axle to it just increases the likelihood of breaking or bending something. Many manufacturers even brag about

how their 4x4s ride like cars (certainly not something we look for in a 4x4), suggesting that the strength of the driveline and suspension is questionable for off-road duty. Lift kits for these 4x4s are usually a sea of brackets and bolts that resembles a jigsaw puzzle or a colorfully painted scrap yard.

Since two-wheel drives don't have transfer cases, front differentials, or front driveshafts to lower or worry about, the lift kits tend to be less bracket-happy. Many of the kits add wheel travel to the front suspension.

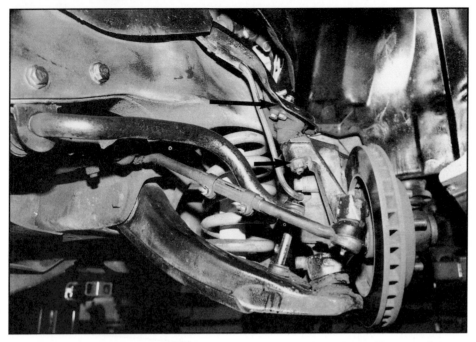

This looks mostly stock but it actually has the makings of a basic 3-inch lift on a coil A-arm truck. Larger coils, ball-joint spacers (arrow) and longer shocks make up the kit. Basic torsion bar lifts are similar. Lift spindles cannot be used with these kits.

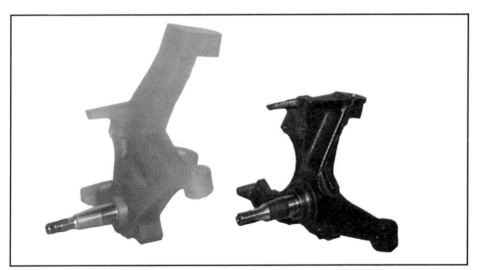

On the left is a model of Fabtech's new 3 1/2-inch lift spindle for '88-'98 GM trucks. Check out the beef compared to the stock piece on the right. The lift is obtained by changing the position of the spindle in relation to the ball joints.

This is a closeup of one of Fabtech's ball-joint spacers. These are mounted on top of the upper ball joints to correct camber on lifted A-arm trucks.

This is something the 4x4 IFS lift manufacturers can't readily do without replacing or modifying the CV joints in the halfshafts (not cheap).

Have Speed, Wheel Travel

If you've decided to actually use your two-by in the dirt, you'll want to look for a kit that offers additional wheel travel. Without a low-range and a front drive axle you're going to have to hit obstacles at speed. The extra wheel travel will absorb the bumps and keep the truck in one piece and on the trail. Of course, you won't be traversing the same bolder-strewn trails as a rock buggy, but you can still have some off-road fun and then drive your truck back to civilization and work the next day.

Often the added wheel travel and speed produces heat in the shocks. Heat causes the shocks to fade and the vehicle to become bouncy and difficult to control. Duals, triples, and more are used to distribute the load and dissipate heat. A shock with a single-tube design will dissipate heat better than other types. Off-road race teams have been using large-diameter reservoir shocks for several years. These shocks are designed and progressively valved for high-speed abuse and won't fade under most circumstances. Only recently has the technology become more affordable from companies like King Off-Road Racing Shocks. These large-diameter shocks generally come in build-your-own-mount lengths, so shock hoops will need to be built to accommodate them. They can also be converted to coilovers if desired. Many manufacturers and custom fabricators offer bolt-on hoops to allow the use of multiple conventional shocks.

A-Arm Suspensions

Two-wheel-drive A-arm suspensions are all very similar. The difference lies in how they are sprung.

Stepping up in cost and performance is the upper arm and coil lift kit. These kits generally increase wheel travel a couple of inches for improved handling off-road. Similar kits are offered for torsion bar trucks.

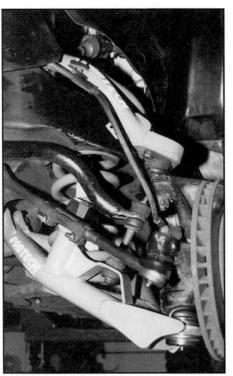

At the top of the heap is the complete upper and lower A-arm and coil kit. This Fabtech setup offers 3 inches of lift and 12 inches of wheel travel. More than 6 inches of lift is obtained when the setup is used with lift spindles.

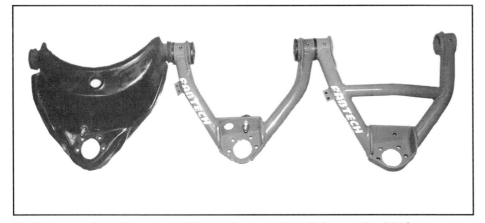

Here's a comparison of upper arms. The stock, stamped-steel piece on the right is more prone to bending than the tubular, chrome-moly arm in the middle. The long-travel upper arm has an extra tube and a gusset wrapped around the ball-joint mounting plate. Also notice the length differences.

Torsion bars or coils can be used to provide rebound to the suspension. All Chevy and Dodge two-bys use coils. The '97–present Ford F-150s, Toyota Tacomas and Tundras, and '98–present Rangers also use coils and A-arms. Torsion bars can be found on '79–'95 Toyota pickups and all Nissans, as well as other imports.

The popularity and total number manufactured of each truck is considered before a company produces a lift for a vehicle. Often the popularity of past models is enough to spark interest in lift production. In this aspect the two-wheel lift market is no different than the 4x4 market. Some trucks have vast options when it comes to lift shopping, while others may be left for the lowered truck crowd.

Coil–A-Arm

Basic: The basic suspension lift for a coil-sprung A-arm truck is a set of lifted coils (up to 3 inches) and ball-joint spacers to correct the camber of the front tires. This type of kit generally doesn't offer an increase in wheel travel or performance. The typical street truck is built in this fashion. The aftermarket coils and shocks provide a firmer ride than factory. This is perhaps the cheapest way to safely lift your coil-sprung two-by.

Basic II: A spindle (knuckle) lift is also very low in the hierarchy of lift systems. Most spindle lifts are 3 inches. A replacement knuckle is used to provide lift. Much like a lowering knuckle, a lifted one has a relocated wheel-bearing spindle to provide the height change. Lift spindles do not provide any performance gains and give the same ride as stock. They merely lift the vehicle to provide room for larger tires. This makes them very popular with the street crowd. The stock shocks are often retained but they should be replaced with firmer units to control the larger tires. Spindle lifts are more expensive than the coil swap and ball-joint spacer kits.

Upper Arms: Next in line are a coil swap and new upper control arms. Longer shocks are usually required for this system. The new upper arms provide proper caster and in most cases an additional 1 or 2 inches of

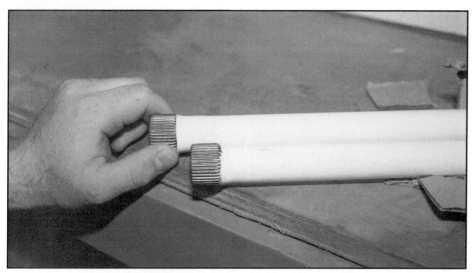

This is a set of aftermarket torsion bars we found at Fabtech. The diameter of the replacement bars is greater than that of the factory pieces. Bigger torsions mean increased spring rate, firmer ride, and less susceptibility to sagging. For really abusive drivers, 300M torsions are available.

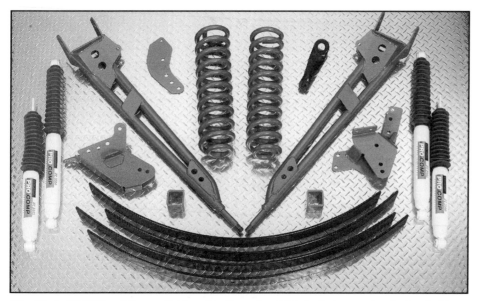

This Stage II F-150 and Bronco lift from Pro-Comp is a fairly typical example of a bracket-type lift with longer radius arms. The factory I-beam pivot brackets and coils are removed from the frame and replaced with the Pro-Comp pieces. This kit retains the original radius arm mounts but they need to be relocated 15 inches back to accommodate the new longer arms. A dropped pitman arm is required and rear add-a-leaves bring up the rear.

additional damping. Lift spindles can be used with these kits to provide even more clearance.

Torsion–A-Arm

Cheap vehicles equipped with torsion bar A-arm suspension can usually be lifted without purchasing parts. Cranking the torsion bars can provide a small lift. By doing this you are preloading the bars and effectively increasing the spring rate. This will firm up the ride and you will lose downtravel but gain uptravel. This can also cause the ride to be rough. If the bars are tightened too much they will eventually sag and need to be replaced. Some vehicles will not align with the torsions overly tightened.

Cheap II: The next cheapest step is to replace the torsions with a set that has a higher spring rate. The benefits and drawbacks are the same as cranking the stock torsions. However, the aftermarket pieces have a bigger diameter and can handle more abuse and lift without sagging.

Army: Upper control arm kits are available for the torsion bar suspensions much like the coil A-arm trucks. The benefits and drawbacks are the same as the coil trucks. If you use the truck off-road it is a good idea to install heavier torsions. For street use, the stock pieces will work fine as long as the bumpstops are positioned in the proper locations. No spindles are available for these trucks.

Big Inch: Few long-travel torsion bar suspensions are available. The truck that enjoys the most number of kits is the '84-'95 Toyota. New upper and lower arms along with a sturdier strut frame provide up to 12 inches of travel. Most multiple shock mounts for this truck are weld-on pieces.

wheel travel. Some trucks will require bumpstop relocation. This type of kit is perhaps the least you should consider if you plan to use your truck in the dirt. Most of these kits provide 2 1/2 to 3 inches of lift. Lift spindles can be used in conjunction with the arms and coils to provide additional lift.

Full-Tilt: At the top of the bolt-on food chain are the upper and lower replacement arm and coil kits. These provide wheel travel up to 12 inches for severe use. The arms increase the track width of the front end and may require the use of fiberglass fenders or fender trimming to provide room for the tires at full stuff. Bolt-on engine-cage shock-hoops are available and afford mounting for dual shocks and

Ford Rangers and '80-'96 F-150s may need these adjustable camber bushings to correct alignment after lifting. They can also be used to increase or decrease caster if need be.

I-Beam

Ford had no idea of the potential of its I-beam suspension when it was first introduced in 1966. Right off the lot the I-beam trucks didn't have much more travel than the A-arm trucks. However, the I-beam suspension is easier and cheaper to lift. Soft coil springs and the lever action provided by the beam made for a great off-road design. From the early '80s to the mid '90s, I-beam suspensions could be found on just about every successful race truck. Even today, most serious prerunners and play trucks use some form of I-beam suspension for its durability, simplicity, and long wheel travel potential. I-beams do have their Achilles heel, though. With the long travel comes excessive amounts of camber and caster change throughout the suspension cycle. This can cause erratic handling if the steering linkages are not considered.

From 1966 to 1979 Ford used the longest equal-length I-beams of any year on its two-wheel-drive F-series trucks. These arms stretched all the way to the opposite framerails. The longer the beams are, the more travel that can be obtained. From 1980 to

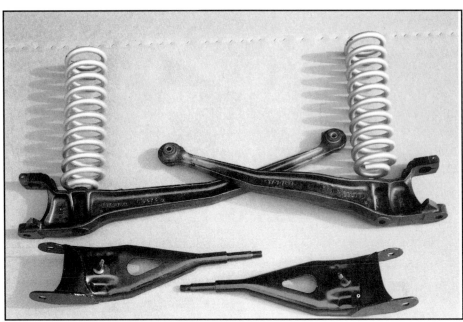

This is the basic bent and aligned beam kit from Autofab for a Ranger. Longer coils provide 4 inches of lift, properly bent beams keep the track width near stock, and modified stock radius arms provide the proper caster. This type of kit is perhaps the easiest to install on the I-beam Fords. No drop pitman arm is required.

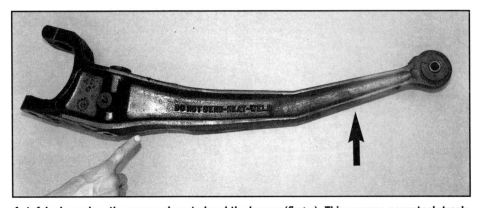

Autofab showed us the proper place to bend the beams (finger). This assures near-stock track-width and strength. Some hacks bend the beams at the small end (arrow). It's easier to do but at the expense of strength and track width. You'll notice the beam says "do not heat or bend." Autofab believes they are plenty strong for normal use. For more abusive conditions the earlier forged nodular iron beams should be used. These beams do not have the warning label and are significantly stronger.

1996 Ford used unequal-length I-beams, the driver side being longer. This allows the driver side to provide more travel than the passenger side with less camber change. Needless to say, this can cause some unique handling situations. The '99–present Super Duty trucks also use unequal length I-beams.

Rangers (and Bronco IIs) from 1983 to 1997 also enjoy the long travel

benefits of I-beam suspension. Much like the '80–'96 fullsizes, the Rangers have a longer beam on the driver side. Rangers are one of the most popular two-wheel-drive trucks to lift, and understandably so. You could get one with a speedy 4.0 V-6 and the same 8.8 rear axle (narrowed) that came in the full sizes. Match this with the long wheel travel and the relatively low price and high availability of these

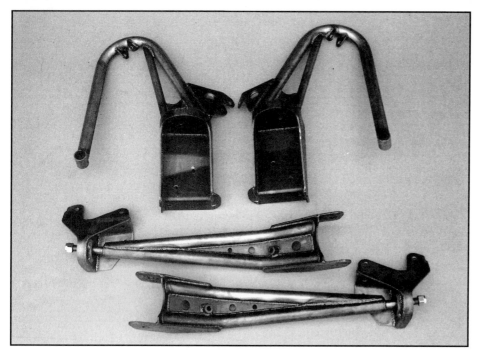

Adding Autofab's longer radius arms (bottom) and long travel coil-bucket shock hoops (top) to a bent beam kit will net you up to 15 inches of wheel travel. Lots of travel is the key to a successful two-by.

Fabtech offers production-built chrome-moly I-beams for Rangers and F-150s. These beams provide gobs of wheel travel and up to 8 inches of lift when all of the corresponding parts are used.

trucks and you've got yourself a runner. Explorers have a similar design but the parts are not interchangeable.

Stuff It In: The simplest method used to lift coil-sprung I-beam suspensions is installing a larger coil. This can provide up to 2 inches of lift.

Some vehicles will not align when set up this way. Adjustable camber bushings can be used to correct alignment in some cases. Coils that provide more than 2 inches of lift can be used if alignment is not a concern as in tough-truck racing.

Stack-it Bracket: Complete bracket

lift kits can be used to lift an I-beam truck. These kits are the same kits used for the 4x4 versions of the trucks ('83–'97 Rangers or '80–'96 fullsizes). The factory I-beams and radius arms are retained but lowered with bolt-on brackets. These lifts don't really enhance performance so they should be left for the street crowd. They are available in lifts up to 8 inches. Installation can be a pain since it requires the removal of several large frame rivets, which are replaced with bolts.

Stack-it Bracket Plus: These kits are often the same ones as the bracket kits except that they come with longer replacement radius arms. Thicker brackets are sometimes used as well. This type of kit is the least you should consider if you are planning to hit the dirt. The longer radius arms increase wheel travel and help keep caster change to a minimum during suspension cycling. They also help triangulate and strengthen the suspension assembly. The kits are often referred to as second stage, or Class II, indicating some superiority. They provide 2-3 inches of wheel travel over stock.

Get Bent: Bending or aligning the I-beams for larger coils is a very common practice. Usually 4-inch coils are used but often you can fit 6-inch units, depending on the vehicle. Bending the beams should be done by someone who has experience. An incorrect procedure can cause the beams to fail or make the vehicle impossible to align. One drawback of bending the beams is that the track width of the front end becomes narrower than stock. The radius arms need to be modified for proper caster or, better yet, replaced with longer pieces. This method of lifting affords

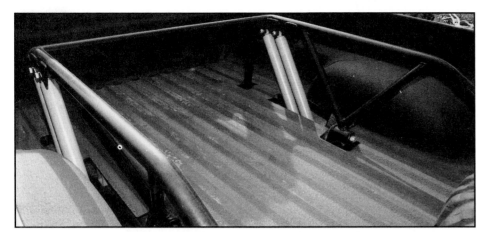

For the rear, Autofab offers bed cages with shock mounts and optional spare tire carriers (not shown). The systems provide up to 18 inches of travel when set up with quality springs.

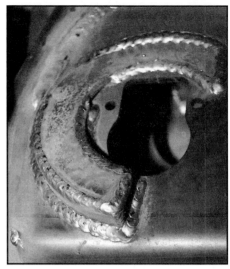

Quality costs. Look for quality components when purchasing a kit that you intend to use off-road. Clean welds and almost art-like fabrication like this is what to look for. Other lifts with less meticulous fabrication and sloppy welds covered in 90 coats of paint should not be considered off-road friendly.

more wheel travel and strength than the bracket kits. Many manufacturers offer bent beams and modified radius arms in a kit that you supply cores for. These kits can provide up to 15 inches of travel if used in conjunction with bolt-on or custom shock towers.

New Beams: Climbing up the I-beam suspension ladder brings us to production built beams. Although they're not one-off creations, they're still not cheap. The beams are usually made from chrome-moly tubing or plate. Their design allows them to accommodate up to an 8-inch lift coil. Longer radius arms are required for these beams but all the components are bolt-on. Huge amounts of travel up to and beyond 15 inches is possible depending on the shock towers. The static track width that these beams provide is usually a few inches more than stock. When the suspension compresses, the track width will be several inches wider than stock. Fiberglass or trimmed fenders may be necessary to provide full use of the travel.

Custom Fab

As with any hobby or sport, sometimes you just can't buy exactly what you want because it isn't available. The same is true when building

two-wheel-drive suspensions. For extreme-duty, no-holds-barred abuse, you'll need to talk to a custom fabricator. Tell him what you want, and get enrolled in his direct deposit banking. Fabrication work isn't cheap but the outcome is usually just what you wanted or more than you expected. Long-travel A-arms, extra long I-beams, coilover shocks, chrome-moly tubing and gussets, and more are not out of the realm of possibility. If you're building a truck

like this, seriously consider a full rollcage from bumper to bumper. Not only will you thank us if you ever need it, but a well-built cage will make the frame more rigid and less prone to bending and breaking.

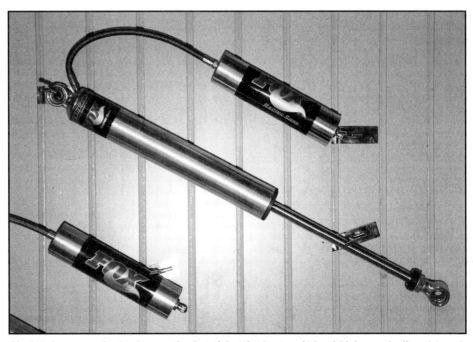

Single-tube reservoir shocks are the hot ticket for long periods of high-speed off-road travel. Standard shocks generally fade within minutes, while these can go practically all day.

11

Two-by-Four, Part 1

Building a Three Link and Converting Two-Wheel Drive to Four-Wheel Drive

By John Cappa
Photography by John Cappa

If you have a two-wheel drive and you're fed up with getting stuck, or your buddies with four-bys just plain leave you in the dust, then it's probably time to sell the pegleg, step up to the plate, and buy a 4x4. Or is it?

Two-bys can be lots of fun for high-speed use, and our '79 Ford F-150 was no exception. It certainly wasn't a slouch with 35-inch tires and 17 inches of travel in the front, accompanied by 14 inches in the rear. Jumps from 5 feet were no problem, and dips and bumps were easily absorbed. However, dune and mud runs had left us stranded and wanting a 4x4. In some situations low range would have been nice too. We have a lot of time and money wrapped up in our truck,

including a new engine, tranny, and rearend. It didn't make much sense to sell it and start over, so we decided to convert it to a 4x4. It is possible to buy a 4x4 of the same make and bolt on all of the good parts and sell the leftover truck, but we just couldn't part with our '79.

Planning

Now that we decided to keep the truck, we needed to decide how to go about the conversion. Bolting on factory '73–'79 Ford 4x4 components (tranny, transfer case, axle, and suspension) might seem like the easiest method, and it is for many models. It turns out that the '66–'79 Ford two-wheel-drive frames are

different from the four-wheel-drive frames. The main difference is the engine crossmember. The 4x4 crossmember is made from square tube and is positioned in front of the engine, away from the axle assembly. The two-wheel-drive piece provides a mounting location for the I-beams and hangs below the engine. It needs to be removed or modified unless a huge lift is planned. We were lifting our truck 6–7 inches over stock.

Another complication is that the transmission in your two-wheel drive is probably fine. This was the case for our truck, so it seemed wasteful to swap it out for a 4x4 trans mated to a transfer case. A divorce-mounted transfer case was the perfect solution.

This is how our front suspension started. We didn't reuse any of the two-wheel-drive components so the installation would be the same if the truck is stock or lifted. The steering linkage and box is behind the I-beams on two-wheel-drive '66–'79 Ford F-100s, F-150s, and F-250s. The suspensions are almost identical on these trucks as well.

Our Dana 44 came rebuilt from Boyce Equipment. New calipers, locking hubs, freshly turned rotors, and a new tie rod and ends were only some of the features. It also came in a fresh gloss-black skin.

We swung the 44 under the frame after removing all of the two-wheel-drive components and marked where the crossmember needed to be notched. The crossmember could be removed and replaced with a smaller unit, but the motor mounts are attached to it so we decided that notching it was the best solution for clearance.

This is how we notched the front portion of the crossmember. The differential now has room to fit up inside the channeled factory crossmember. The backside is also clearanced for the pinion and one of the links.

Divorced Dana 24s and NP205s are somewhat common in wrecking yards and can be found relatively cheap since they hardly ever break. A divorce mounted case would also help with weight distribution by moving a good portion of bulk to the rear of the vehicle. The third advan-tage that came to mind was that we could clock the transfer case for more ground

clearance. We didn't need an expensive adapter, just a third driveshaft. We decided on a divorced Dodge NP205 to provide splitting duties.

The Dodge transfer case has the front output on the passenger side. This offers us plenty of options for a front axle but we have our limitations too. Custom units were too expensive

and we wanted to be able to buy spare parts from wrecking yards if need be. Ford axles have the differentials on the wrong side, and the high-pinion design would have caused major

What It Will Take

If you think you're up to the task of fabricating a similar front suspension, but you're not sure what tools, parts, or materials you'll need, we've made a shopping list for you. Some items may not be necessary, but this will depend on the vehicle you're working with and the type of brackets and shock hoops you decide to build. Needless to say, you should be extremely proficient with all of these tools before you remove the first bolt.

Necessary Tools

Common hand tools
- Angle finder
- Assorted files
- Assorted drill bits and hole saws
- Grinder
- Welder (preferably MIG or TIG) with at least 1/4-inch single-pass capability
- Sawzall, torch, or plasma cutter
- Chop saw
- Extra-tall jackstands
- Ratchet straps

Optional Tools

- Tube bender: can be used to make cool shock hoops and brackets
- Tubing notcher: copes tubing for easy fit-up and welding
- 3/4-inch fine thread tap

Materials

- 3/16-inch mild plate steel: size and amount will depend on bracket design
- 1 1/2-inch 0.120 wall mild steel tubing: 15-30 feet
- 1 1/8-inch DOM tubing with 5/8-inch inside diameter: 4 feet
- 1 1/2-inch heavy-wall DOM or chrome moly tubing: amount depends on the length of the links
- 1 1/8-inch heavy-wall DOM with 11/16-inch inside diameter: length will depend on drag link and Panhard rod design

Parts

- Wrangler shackle bushings (two pair)
- PFTE- (Teflon) lined Aurora rod ends (size and type will depend on use)
- King Prerunner coilover and standard shocks and hardware
- Eibach coils
- Divorced Dodge NP205
- '72-'76 1/2-ton GM Dana 44 front axle
- '73-'79 F-150 hubs and rotors
- Skyjacker stainless braided lines
- Warn locking hubs
- Miscellaneous Grade 8 hardware
- Autofab 4 1/2-inch bumpstops
- Flaming River steering shaft
- GM 800 steering box with Camaro pitman arm
- Driveshafts
- Transfer case shift linkage
- Wheels and tires
- Lift for rear

clearance problems with the factory two-wheel-drive crossmember. Chevy axles have the diff on the same side as the Dodge transfer case and are more common than Dodge axles with 5-on-5 1/2 lug patterns. So Chevy it was.

We thought that a bombproof Dana 60 would be nice, but we doubted that its size and weight were really needed. In fact, it was too heavy and probably way overkill for our high-speed, nimble truck with 35-inch tires. It was also an expensive option that would need to be converted to a five-

lug or we would have to swap out the rear axle to match the eight-lug front. A Dana 44 from a '73–'76 Chevy was deemed to be the best option. It has 1/2-inch-thick, 2 3/4-inch-diameter axletubes, the diff is on the correct side, lots of them exist in wrecking yards, and the six-lug pattern could be easily changed to 5-on-5 1/2. It turned out that the width was only slightly wider than the factory Ford 9-inch in the back of our truck. A call to Boyce Equipment netted us a rebuilt Dana 44 with 4.10 gears to match the back. If

your project or budget calls for a 10-bolt, a Dana 60, or even a 2 1/2 or a 5-ton axle, Boyce has them all.

Suspension

The truck was originally built as a high-speed desert runner, and we didn't want to lose that capability with the integration of four-wheel drive. Leaf springs would have been simple to install since the perches on our axle were about the same width as our framerails. Coils could have been mounted in the original (aftermarket

The lower-link brackets are made from 3/16-inch mild steel, 1 1/2-inch 0.120 wall tubing, and heavy-wall 5/8-inch inside diameter DOM tubing. They are located on the frame using holes that had been stamped into the frame at the factory. This ensures that the brackets are mounted in the correct positions.

We built our own threaded tubing adapters, but they can be purchased from circle track and drag race suppliers. We used a 3/4-inch tap to thread short sections of heavy-wall DOM tubing for our adapters.

Flaming River supplied a collapsible double-D shaft with U-jointed ends that fit our GM steering box. The Ford column was cut and ground to match the double-D joint.

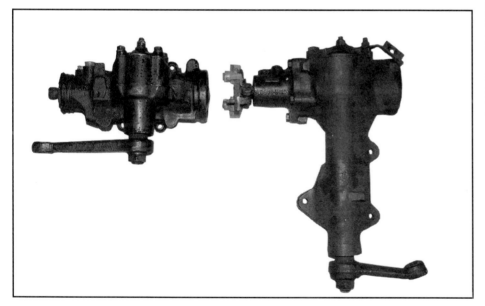

The factory Ford two-wheel-drive steering box (right) has a grotesquely long sector shaft that can snap if abused. We moved the steering-box mount to a position in front of the axle and used a common GM car box (left).

in our case) coil buckets, but installing Ford radius arms on our Chevy axle posed its own set of problems. Neither of these designs would look or perform any different than a normal straight-axle Ford 4x4. Also, if long travel is built into the factory radius arm suspension there will be significant caster change throughout the travel. Articulation would also be limited by the presence of the C-bushings. We knew it would be difficult to keep the 17 inches of suspension we originally had and still maintain safe steering linkages, but we were willing to settle for a little less travel in exchange for four-wheel drive.

We chose to build a three-link suspension with a Panhard rod. Coilover shocks will compactly and economically perform damping and rebound chores. The links are attached to the axle and frame with Aurora rod ends on 1 1/2-inch DOM tubing. The tubing has a wall thickness of almost 3/8 inch so it can handle rocks and just about anything we hit it with. All three arms are the same length, and the upper and lower arms are parallel to each other. This ensures that there is no caster change throughout the travel and we only

47

All three links are cut to the same length and the mounts are tack-welded to the axle. The links are mounted parallel so there is no caster change during suspension cycling.

With everything tack-welded and mocked up, we then cycled the suspension to see what would hit where. The bumpstop positions are located with this information.

again, only one spare is needed.

Staying true to the find-it-anywhere motif, we ditched the behind-the-engine steering and chose a '70–'78 Camaro Saginaw power steering box that has 2 1/2 turns lock-to-lock. The box is a 76 GM 800 unit with the larger bearings and stronger casting. This box has the same bolt pattern as many American cars, so a field replacement should be a snap if it should ever fail. The box is connected to our factory column with a Flaming River collapsible steering shaft. We built our own steering-box mount using DOM tubing that pierces the freshly reinforced framerail.

In this chapter, we'll cover the axle installation, steering, and the three-link suspension design. In the next

need to carry one spare arm. The axle is kept inline by a 1 1/8-inch-diameter, heavy wall DOM Panhard rod with Aurora rod ends. The drag link is made of the same material. Both components use the same rod ends and both are the same length, so

chapter, we'll cover the transfer case, driveshafts, the shocks, how to build the shock hoops, and any leftover details.

Once all of the mounts were positioned where we wanted them we removed the axle for finish welding. It's best to weld small sections at a time to keep the housing from distorting.

The threaded ends are welded to the ends of the links, and they have two rosette or plug welds for additional strength. We removed the Aurora rod ends before welding to keep them from being damaged during the welding process.

We built our crossmember using 1 1/2-inch 0.120 wall tubing. The upper link is bolted to this component. The transfer case shifters and the transmission will also be mounted to this structure.

The Autofab 4 1/2-inch urethane bumpstops should only be compressed to about half their height. Building the bumpstop mounts so that metal contacts metal at full bump eliminates the possibility of over-compressing and damaging the urethane. A loud clank can be heard when we get too crazy, which lets us know we need to slow down.

To convert our Chevy axle to a five-lugger we called 4 Wheel Parts Wholesalers and ordered new hubs and rotors for a '73–'79 F-150. The Chevy wheel bearings and calipers fit the Ford components. We added Warn locking hubs and Skyjacker vinyl-coated stainless steel brake lines.

This is the almost complete steering and suspension. The tie rod is made from 1 1/2-inch 0.120 wall tubing. Aurora rod ends cinched with Grade 8 hardware allow movement at all pivot points. The drag link and Panhard rod are almost parallel—and they're the same length—so bumpsteer was minimal when we cycled the suspension.

Having become fed up with sticking our two-by in the dunes and mud, we decided that it was time to get some extra wheels spinning. Very few of us can afford to drop a truck off at a fab shop and leave a blank check, so we are doing all of the fabrication and design ourselves. We know that many of you have welders and other fabricating tools and are fairly proficient with them, so this project shouldn't seem so far out of reach.

In the last chapter, we covered how to build the three-link suspension, the solid front-axle installation, steering, and the initial planning of our two-wheel-drive to four-wheel-drive conversion on our '79 Ford F-150. The design of the three-link is such that it can be done on any straight front-axle vehicle if you don't mind doing a little homework. In this chapter, we'll cover how to build the shock hoops for coilover and standard long-travel shocks. We'll finish off next chapter with the transfer case installation, and tie up the other loose ends.

We often see coilover and large-diameter, reservoired shocks on the trail. A few years ago this was almost unheard of. The industry has since realized that there is a market for quality budget shocks. King Shocks is well known throughout the off-road race scene as one of the best custom shock manufacturers. King builds full-tilt, wonder-budget race shocks, but it also offer the Pre-Runner Series shocks for significantly less coin. We provided King with a good idea of what the truck weighed, its intended use, and the mounting locations of the shocks. With this information the company assembles and valves the shocks for the specific application. These could be the last shocks you ever buy because they can be rebuilt and revalved if you decide to use them in a different application. The standard Pre-Runners can be converted to a coilover by adding the threaded adjusting sleeve and other hardware.

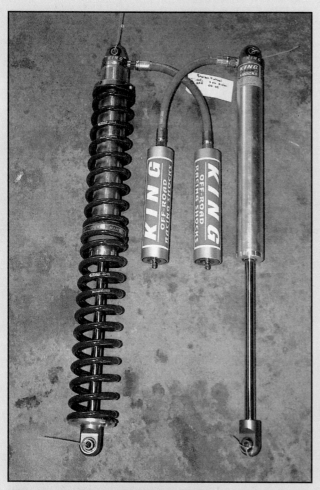

With King's help we decided that the 14-inch-travel Pre-Runners were the best choice for our project. The front shock (left) has the coil hardware and Eibach coils installed.

Eibach offers a number of different coils categorized by spring rate and length. The coil on the right is rated at 500 pounds per inch, while the other is a 200-pound spring. Notice the difference in thickness of the coil wire. King recommended dual-rate coils. The lower coils on our shocks are 350-pound and the uppers are 250-pound. This is considered a light setup and should put the shock in the middle of its travel with the static weight of our truck.

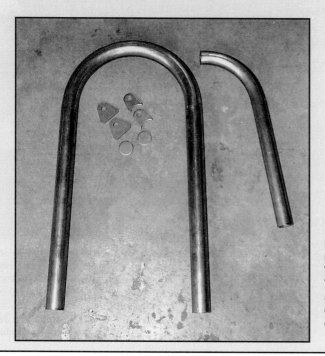

In addition to the tools mentioned in the last chapter, you will need the raw materials shown here to build the shock hoops. The main part of the hoop is 1 3/4-inch, 0.120-inch wall tubing. The brace is 1 1/2-inch, 0.120-inch wall tubing. The weld tabs are stamped units from A&A Manufacturing. A fabricator or an exhaust shop should be able to bend the tubing for you if you don't have a bender.

In order to keep the shocks from bottoming at full bump we removed the urethane bumpstops and let the axle rest metal-on-metal before fabricating the hoops. We also removed one of the coils to ease full compression of the shock. One coil is left in place to expose any clearance problems.

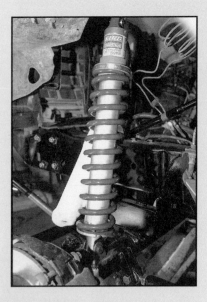

The main hoop is welded to the frame with 2 1/2-inch sections of 1 3/4-inch tubing. The caps from A&A are welded from the inside for a clean look. Notice the tight fit of the pieces before they are welded.

This is what the front hoop looks like from the engine compartment. We'll add a removable crossover brace that will stabilize the front hoops once the engine is in place.

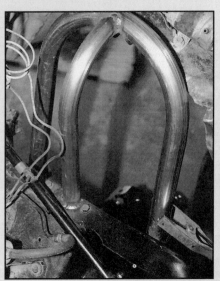

The shocks can be adjusted for the desired height once they are installed. Tightening the adjusters or swapping to a stiffer coil (not longer) will lift the vehicle. The adjusters always have to have some preload to keep the coils in place. Lowering the vehicle will usually require a lighter set of coils. The reservoirs and shocks should be mounted away from heat sources for best performance.

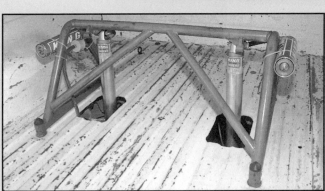

In the rear we replaced our dual conventional shocks with single, non-coilover, reservoired Kings mounted to our existing bed cage. We decided long ago that we didn't mind the shocks coming through the bed. The cage bolts directly to the frame through the body-mount bolts. The reservoirs have been temporarily fastened with zip ties until we build some real mounts. King offers anodized, billet aluminum reservoir clamps for those looking for a real clean trick look.

Two-by-Four, Part 3

Driveline and Airtime

By John Cappa
Photography by John Cappa and Christian Hazel

13

We originally planned to have our pre-runnin' two-wheel-drive '79 Ford F-150 totally converted to a whumpin' four-wheel drive in three parts. We did it, sorta. If you haven't been following along we began the conversion in chapter 11 by cutting off the original front suspension, choosing an axle and transfer case, building a three-link front suspension, and designing a steering system. We continued in chapter 12 with the coilover shocks and their mounting. What we have here is the completion of the project and some tips about what we would like to change and the stuff we'll live with.

Transfer Case

Our original transmission was fine and had less than 5,000 miles on it since a rebuild. We have no idea how automatics work and we don't want to know, so we decided that a divorced transfer case was the perfect way to keep from tearing into the tranny. We called Boyce Equipment and ordered a divorced Dodge NP205. This version of the NP205 has four 5/8-inch, coarse-thread holes tapped in the top of the housing that make building a mount easy. We used 1 1/2-inch 0.120-wall tubing for the main structure and 1-inch DOM tubing with a 5/8-inch hole to firmly secure four 5/8-inch bolts to the transfer case.

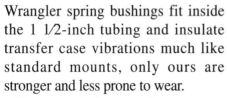

Wrangler spring bushings fit inside the 1 1/2-inch tubing and insulate transfer case vibrations much like standard mounts, only ours are stronger and less prone to wear.

To support the transfer case, we boxed one crossmember for strength and added mounting ears to it. It was originally used to support one end of the second (now removed) fuel tank. The other mount bolts to the side of the framerail. You may need to fabricate crossmembers depending on your application and where you mount the transfer case. The biggest advantage to using a divorced transfer case on our Ford was the ability to clock it without a custom adapter. This gave us extra ground clearance under the already-low transfer case. However, the oil filler needed to be extended up with a short section of pipe to provide proper lubrication.

The dotted line indicates the oil level with the transfer case mounted in the factory application.

Driveshafts

Since our NP205 was originally from a 1-ton, it came with monster 1350-series yokes on the input and rear output, while the front output is a 1310 series. We called Tom Wood's Custom Driveshafts and gave the company our measurements for all three driveshafts (don't forget about the nubby unit between the transmission and transfer case).

We also found out that we could have our shafts painted almost any color at no extra charge. Just to test that out we went for a powder blue in

hopes that it would match the anodizing on the shocks. It didn't. We did have to clearance the rear 1350 yoke and driveshaft with a grinder to keep all 14 inches of rear wheel travel bind-free.

What We Want to Change (Already)

• We had thought the Camaro steering box was a bit too twitchy for our Ford. It turns out that the rod-ended tie rods twist, allowing some wandering in the steering. Installing a steering arm on the passenger-side knuckle and a longer drag link should solve the problem.

• The suspension cycles fine but we feel a longer track bar and drag link

(ours are 36 inches long) would make it handle better (less side-to-side axle movement when cycling).

• We would like the truck to sit 3 inches lower and still have plenty of uptravel. To do this we would need to remove the original engine cross-member and possibly build new motor mounts. If you want to run 40-inch tires or larger this modification is not needed.

Dealin' with It

• There is a vibration coming from the nubby driveshaft. We tried shimming the tranny and transfer case and it's better, but we still feel the vibration at 50–60 mph. We'll eventually change the transfer case mounts so the divorced driveshaft has correct angles.

• The transfer case probably hangs down too low for rockcrawling but it's fine for bashing around trails and general off-road mayhem.

Shifting

After eyeballing an exploded diagram of an NP205 we decided that it was possible to safely convert our shifting mechanism to a twin-stick for Atlas-like shifting abilities with bombproof strength. We built a bracket that holds the individual shifters and it bolts to the rear of the transmission. All-thread rod and miniature rod ends from the local hardware store make up the rest of the linkage. The twin sticks pop up through the floor and are sealed with a boot almost like original parts.

What We Changed

The 250-pound over 350-pound coils we originally chose left the truck sitting too high. We swapped them for 150-pound over 250-pound coils.

14 Inside Three Popular Lift Kits

By Christian Hazel
Photography by *4-Wheel & Off-Road* **Staff**

First we asked around to determine the top three vehicle makes people were buying suspension lifts for. Then we tried to unlock the mysteries inherent in lifting these vehicles—you know, the nitty-gritty stuff the salesman may conveniently forget to tell you about. The kit that seems like a screaming deal may not include suspension or steering components you didn't even know were vital. We've tried to compile some info that will help you wade through suspension catalogs and Web pages. Face it. Having a suspension that's tall but doesn't work is as out as waterbeds and naked hippie chicks painted on black velvet.

1973–1987 Leaf Sprung

You couldn't ask for an easier vehicle to lift. Sixteen bolts hold the axles to the springs, and eight bolts hold the springs to the frame. The most popular lift size is 4 inches, but lifts from 2 to 12 inches are available. However, check to see what your lift kit includes. Some systems only include lift springs for the front and blocks or add-a-leaves for the rear. Here are some of the factors that must be addressed.

Steering

When a lift of more than 2 inches is installed, some effort must be made to improve steering geometry. Generally, lifts of 3–4 inches require a dropped pitman arm or a dropped drag link. Lifts of 5–6 inches require a raised steering arm or steering block and perhaps a dropped drag link. Lifts of 8–10 inches require a dropped pitman arm and either a raised steering arm, a dropped drag link, or both. Lifts of more than 10 inches often require some degree of custom work, such as a crossover steering setup to regain any type of steering feel and turning radius.

Springs

Generally, all of the major-brand kits include front lift springs for anything from 2 to 12 inches. You'll want to check if they include bushings and if they're polyurethane or rubber. Most will include the front U-bolts and nuts.

For the rear, many kits use either an add-a-leaf or a lift block to raise the rear. The lowest-priced kit will rarely include a set of replacement rear lift springs.

Installing add-a-leaves requires disassembling the rear spring pack. The leaves may sag over time. They also increase the stiffness of the rear springs, but they can help reduce axlewrap. Lift blocks are extremely cheap and easy to install but may work themselves out in some instances and can contribute to increased axlewrap.

Replacement rear springs are more expensive but are our favorite method by which to lift the rear end. They'll generally resist sagging and axlewrap and, depending on the lift height, may actually improve flex over stock. However, heavily arched lift springs can reduce suspension flex.

Hardware

Most often, lift kits only include the front U-bolts and front spring eye bushings. You'll need longer U-bolts if you're using a lift block and sometimes an add-a-leaf than if you're using a replacement spring pack.

Most Overlooked

Don't assume your kit includes shocks. Often it won't. Expect to pay at least another $100 for shocks.

Longer brake lines or brake-line drop brackets are often needed for lifts over 4 inches. Some kits include the drop brackets, but few include longer brake lines.

If you go taller than 2 inches, you'll most likely need to lower your sway bar. Almost no kits include the brackets or spacers for this, but several manufacturers offer them as an option.

Driveshaft angles become problematic with even the smallest lifts. Most kits include degree wedges attached to their spring packs to improve driveshaft angles. Others require the transfer case to be dropped, which is an extra-cost option not offered by every company. This, however, may put stress on the motor mounts, tilt the fan precariously close to the radiator, and cause increased front driveshaft angles.

Longer driveshafts or driveshafts with a CV joint may need to be installed in lifts over 4–6 inches. Some companies offer driveshaft spacers, but we shy away from using those.

The most common kit sizes for leaf-sprung vehicles are 4 and 6 inches. The 4-inch often requires a dropped pitman arm, while the 6-inch requires a new steering arm (shown).

Lift springs not only put the frame and body farther away from the axle, but they often flex more than stockers. Longer brake lines are usually required to prevent overextension at full droop. This stock line is like a tightrope.

Higher-lift replacement rear springs often have a heavier arc that can pull the shackle forward, out of its ideal position. This is about the only advantage lift blocks have over replacement springs

1988–1998 IFS GM

If the '73–'87 GM trucks are the easiest to lift, then the '88–'98s are among the hardest. Most kits require professional installation, including cutting, grinding, and torching. Lift heights range from 2 to 6 inches. Like the earlier straight-axle GMs, the later IFS models need certain things addressed, like longer brake lines and driveshaft angles. The brackets and steering system are so complicated that most kits arrive in four or five hefty boxes.

Steering

Perhaps the most important thing to consider with IFS kits is the quality of the steering components and to what degree the steering geometry is considered. The good news is that IFS lifts are so complicated that every kit includes steering corrections. That's one reason they're so expensive.

One component you should pay attention to is the idler arm. The idler arm holds one side of the steering center link, while the pitman arm holds the other. The '92-and-up GMs came from the factory with the stronger three-bolt idler arm, but you can upgrade the weaker '88–91 two-bolt idler arm to the stronger three-bolt design or use a heavy-duty Moog unit. Most kits add a second idler arm for more support. This ensures that the centerlink gets the proper support, especially with the added stress of bigger rolling stock.

Springs

Most IFS kits retain the stock torsion bars. Larger-diameter torsion bars are available, but, like thicker leaf springs, they offer a higher spring rate and are usually used in rigs with winches or heavy front ends. Shorter kits simply raise the rear of the vehicle with blocks and depend on cranking the torsion bars for more lift in front. However, the better short kits and all the tall kits employ lowering brackets to raise the frame and body away from the suspension.

As with '73–'87 GMs, the rear of these vehicles are usually lifted via blocks or an add-a-leaf, but replacement rear springs are also available.

Hardware

Like the earlier GMs, most kits don't include rear U-bolts and nuts unless they employ a rear lift block.

Most Overlooked In some cases, the cans (or reservoirs) of the shocks will hit suspension components, so the shocks must be mounted upside down for clearance. Make sure the shock is a type that functions properly upside down.

An alignment is not optional. You must have the vehicle aligned as soon as possible to return the caster, camber, and toe to tolerable specs.

You will need to make $50–$75 in exhaust modifications for front driveshaft clearance.

You will need to notch the differential for component clearance on some kits.

With some kits that use ball joint spacers, wheels need at least 3¾ inches of backspacing. Factory wheels will not work.

Your truck will not drive and handle the same as it did stock. You've modified your whole front suspension geometry and range of motion. It's not going to behave like a stock vehicle.

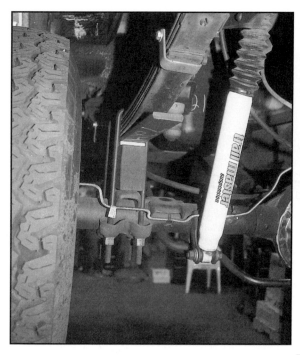

This dropped centerlink helps keep the tie rods in phase with the lower control arms. It's also important to make sure the centerlink has plenty of support via an additional idler arm like this Trail Master unit has.

Rears are most commonly lifted via a rear lift block (shown) or an add-a-leaf. Replacement rear springs are an extra-cost option.

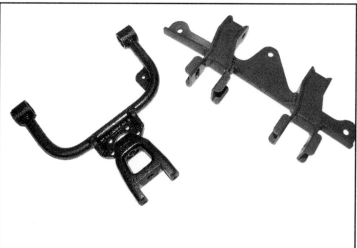

Two different schools. On the left is the replacement upper control arm and ball joint spacer, which require wheels with at least 3 3⁄4 inches of backspacing. In effect, it's like adding a lengthened knuckle. On the right is the drop bracket, which utilizes the stock control arm and ball joint and allows the use of stock wheels.

Brackets are used to relocate the torsion bars to a lower point on the frame (above, left) and also to relocate the lower arms (above, right).

1980–1996 Ford Twin Traction Beam (TTB)

It's pretty much only the factory suspension you can easily tweak 10 inches or more of travel from. When the Ford TTB front axle design debuted in 1980 it was unique—in the 4WD market, that is. Lift heights range from 1 to 8 inches. Kits are available that either retain or replace many of the stock components, so unlike GM IFS kits, a lot of variety can be had. Here are some things to look for.

Steering

As for steering corrections, it's pretty simple. Dropped pitman arms are available in 4- or 5 1/2-inch lift versions. Try to match the pitman arm to the drop brackets as closely as possible. For example, if you're installing a 4-inch lift, ideally you'd use a 4-inch dropped pitman arm. Some creativity will be needed on lifts of 8 inches.

Springs

Coils are bitchin' for tons of droop and compression. Most kits include new front coils of varying heights, but limiting straps should be used to

keep them from overextending. Also, kits of 6 inches or more should use raised bumpstops or bumpstop spacers to prevent cheap springs from compressing too much and flattening out.

Once again, replacement rear lift springs cost extra. The rears of most kits employ single add-a-leaves, progressive dual add-a-leaves, or lift blocks. Fords came from the factory with rear blocks that had built-in bumpstop contacts, so the lift blocks can either be stacked on top of the factory blocks to lower the bumpstops or below the factory blocks to raise the bumpstops. We wouldn't touch either of these setups for a number of reasons, the least of which is that the rear blocks are prone to spitting out under severe use.

Hardware

Like GMs, the Ford kits only include rear U-bolt kits if a rear lift block is being used. Also count on reusing your factory pivot bolts on the beams.

Most Overlooked

Check your radius arm bushings and collars. They're not included in kits and are almost always wasted.

You must have alignment cams installed to regain proper camber at around $150.

Sway-bar relocation components and longer brake lines will be needed for taller kits.

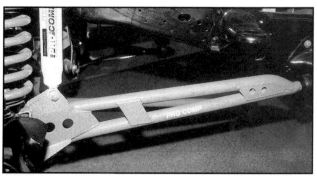

You have two options when it comes to radius arms. The first photo shows a drop bracket used in conjunction with the stock radius arm; the second shows a longer replacement radius arm. The longer arm allows for more suspension travel and a better ride.

The axle pivot brackets lower the beams below the frame. If you just add taller coils without performing this step, the tires would ride on the sidewalls like a cranked VW sandrail.

This is what we mean by stacking blocks to raise or lower bumpstops. Rig-a-jig at its finest.

Skyjacker's 8-Inch Cherokee XJ Lift Kit

15

By Wendy Frazier
Photography by Wendy Frazier

The renovated fire-breathing Cherokee is dressed for trail duty with Mickey Thompson Baja Claw LT305/70s radials paired with M/T Classic II 16x8 wheels. Equipped with "sidebiter" protection, the directional Claws are aggressively treaded to allow for a larger contact area. The circumferential grooves allow for improved flexing when rockcrawling.

For thousands of years, men have marveled at the sight of fire. In the movie *Castaway*, Tom Hanks celebrates on the deserted island by proclaiming, "I have made fire!" Mythological creatures, like Puff the Magic Dragon, are able to breathe fire. We even have friends who pee to extinguish campfires. Ugh. When smoke of Skyjacker's new 8-inch XJ lift began to circulate, we quickly noted the excitement and knew that this would be the ignition of something sizzling.

Mark Hinckley at Off-Road General Store is one of the original sparks when speaking of hot Cherokee transformations. Like jumper cables to a battery, we hooked Hinckley up with Skyjacker. Bolt after bolt, we mused, muscled, and measured. The results that follow are based on our specific application of the new pre-production lift kit for our 2000 Cherokee. We just had to see it to believe it. You know the feeling; it's like staring at the fire for hours.

The largest bolt-on kit on the market

for Cherokee XJs, the Skyjacker 8-inch lift for '89–'01 Cherokees results in out-of-the-box 7 1/4 inches of clearance, 7 1/4 inches of tire stuffing space, and a whole lot more than 7 1/4 inches of suspension articulation. When you add up to 3 inches of tire height—like with our Mickey Thompson Baja Claws and M/T Classic II wheels, you'll roll out of the shop, your buddy's garage, or your driveway with at least 9 inches of "great balls of fire."

Remove the front end equipment, such as tires, shocks, track bars, and steering linkage. Drop the axle and pop out the coils as well. Drill a hole in each lower coil seat and install the aluminum bumpstop spacers. About an inch up the cup you'll see a molded indentation (arrow). Cut there and then install the upper bumpstop.

The new authoritative cow's tongue pitman arm is very "extreme," and keeps the steering in line. Install the new pitman arm.

The exclusive Skyjacker cradle bolts directly to the front differential. The cradle's main purpose is to stabilize the axle and create beefy new control arm mounting brackets. You can't deny that it looks way cool. Fasten the cradle with the U-bolts and the top four diff cover bolts, and attach the front cradle brace.

If you were wowed by the cradle, check out this subframe and transmission crossmember. It's aggressive and stands out like a red-hot chili pepper. The new lower control arms mount to the differential and to the new subframe.

The flat end of the boomerang bracket mounts to the inside of the upper control arm frame mount. This moves the arms down and back. Prepare the new upper control arms by placing a small stepped spacer into each end of the rod end.

With both arms on, finesse the top of the coil in first, then the bottom end, and attach with the retaining clips. Install the track bar, new tie rod, and steering damper.

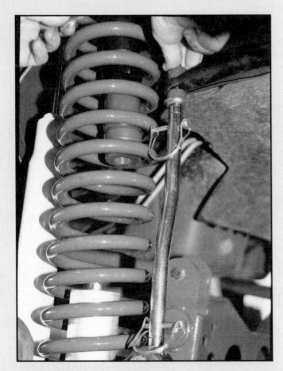

Install the new quick double-disconnect links on the inboard side of the axle bracket, being sure that the offset is turned inward. The pin may interfere with the coil spring, so use a very small piece of duct tape to secure the pin so that it does not interfere with the coil.

Install the extended-length front brake lines and bleed the front brake system. Finally, install new shock absorbers, mount the tires lower to ground, and begin on the rear installation.

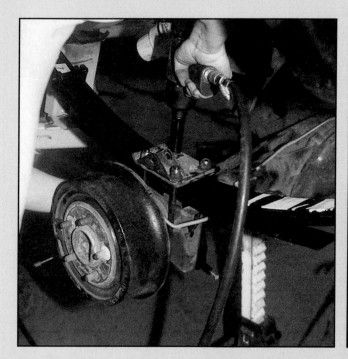

The rear portion of the kit is a piece of cake to install. Remove the rear U-bolts, shocks, springs, and stock shackle, and install the new shackle assemblies. Install the new leaf springs with the thick part of the degree shim facing the rear to rotate the pinion up for driveshaft angles.

Remove the factory bumpstops and fasten the new fire-engine-red bumpstop spacers to the frame and reinstall the mustard-yellow OEM bumpstop to the spacer. Red and yellow are OK for condiments but you won't be eating a hotdog on your bumpstop, so this is where you break out the Krylon and select a color that coordinates.

Install the extended rear brake line and bleed the brake system. Finish the project by installing shocks, checking clearances around the brake lines, and reinstalling the tires, or (hint hint) this may be the time to get the big meats.

Through the Looking Glass—A Quick-Fix List

With any building or modifying project you know to expect curves in the road. Because our kit was pre-production, we knew that we would find these "curves" on our 2000 model install. After thorough testing, our Cherokee reportedly "drives great. The suspension is the softest ride out of all my previous 4x's. And it doesn't have a death wobble." Skyjacker is working to ensure that each kit is a Cherokee owner's dream. You may have a laundry list of your own, but don't worry, the experience will make you the resident suspension "expert."

One final note to those of you who think that your Cherokee is like the General Lee running from Rosco P. Coltrane (P is for Pervis) or if you just like the Duke boys' jumping style, you may run into some trouble with your front driveshaft. The front driveshaft might tag the front of the new crossmember at full droop. Skyjacker has addressed the driveshaft/ crossmember mangle by re-engineering the crossmember for its production kits. Here are a few things we noted during the installation.

The transmission mount bolt pattern was off 7/8 inch, thus the hole did not match up with the crossmember mount. The gang at O.R.G.S. solved the misfit with a spare crossmember mount from a '98 Cherokee. Production kits will have a slot on the new crossmember to account for the variety of Chrysler mount bolt patterns.

The new big and beefy rear lift shackle really is big and beefy. So much so that it snuggles up to the exhaust pipe. Note that this might not happen in your application due to the variety of exhaust bend, but keep your eyes and ears open. A quick clip of about 1 inch off of the exhaust pipe solves the rear clacking.

One of the greatest concerns with lifts of any height is the modification that you may have to make to the other working parts of your vehicle. To address the needs of our Cherokee, we installed a Skyjacker slip-yoke eliminator kit along with a new rear driveshaft to prevent the vehicle from driving like a giddy little girl playing hopscotch. The short shaft kit (slip-yoke eliminator kit) is recommended but not required for installation of the 8-inch kit.

Fitting 35s

With some fender trimming, there is ample space to fit 35-inch tires. You will need a little ingenuity, a steady hand, and some patience. Skyjacker includes a template, details on the how-to, and photographs in its lift instruction packet that comes with the complete kit.

Skyjacker's 6-Inch Cherokee Lift Kit

When a Bit Less Is Just Right

By John Cappa
Photography by John Cappa

16

Okay, so maybe after reading the last chapter you've decided that 8 inches is just too high for your Cherokee. We can't imagine why you might think this, but there is an alternative. It used to be that the only way to get a significant lift on your Cherokee was to stack different kits together. This isn't the ideal setup, but ya gotta do what ya gotta do. Skyjacker offers not only an 8-inch kit, but it also has available their Rock Ready Cherokee kit, which provides a whopping 6 inches of lift right out of the box. And even better—the kit is completely bolt-on. Only four holes need to be drilled, two for the front bumpstops and two for the rear sway bar disconnects.

The kit includes 6-inch coils, 5 1/2-inch Softride rear leaf springs, a heavy-duty subframe assembly with an integrated transfer-case cross-member, new links with monstrous rod ends, a new rod-ended track bar, a dropped pitman arm, bumpstop extensions, front and rear sway-bar disconnects, stainless brake lines, and four Softride shocks. The Rock Ready Cherokee kit offers all the benefits of custom-built components in a bolt-on kit.

With the vehicle properly supported, the factory suspension links, coils, shocks, and so on are removed. A 3/8-inch hole is drilled in each coil bucket for the bumpstop extensions.

With the transmission supported, the factory crossmember is removed and replaced with the Skyjacker subframe and crossmember. This unit bolts to the unibody using the original mounting points.

The original lower stamped steel links with rubber bushings (bottom) are replaced with longer tubular links with rod ends (top). The upper links are also replaced with longer units.

The new coils can be installed without the use of a spring compressor. The front shocks bolt on in the original mounts using the factory hardware.

Short, vulnerable rubber lines are replaced with longer, chaff resistant, polyurethane-coated, stainless steel Skyjacker pieces.

This is the completed frontend with the optional steering stabilizer and heavy-duty tie rod for the driver's side. The new track bar is located just above the original track-bar mount and bolts into the old steering stabilizer mount.

The rear is lifted with new leaf springs and longer shackles with urethane bushings.

At full steering lock our 33x13.50 tires on 15x9 Weld wheels fit with just a bit of trimming to the front valence. We would have been better off with 15x8s and backspacing around 3 1/2–4 inches rather than the 3-inch spacing that our wheels have.

The completed rig fits 33s without stacking kits. The lift will work without a tailshaft conversion on both the two- and four-door models. The wheelbases are the same at 101.4 inches. However, we think that the optional tailshaft conversion is a must-have for any NP231.

The Best Bronco Lift Kit Around

James Duff Goes Long Travel

By Craig Perronne
Photography by Craig Perronne

17

If you are an early Bronco fan then you know one thing—in stock form, your suspension sucks. Short shocks and radius arms seriously hamper efforts to get articulation. Older coil designs give a tank-like ride and zero flex. To make things even worse, no one has yet to offer a complete system that gives loads of articulation. This had made those folks who actually use their Broncos go through the headache-ridden process of custom suspension building that often resulted in ill-working suspensions.

Many Bronco owners have dreamed of a suspension that is easy to install and gives massive gains in articulation. That dream has become reality with the introduction of the James Duff Long Travel System for '66–'77 Broncos. The new system combines the company's Stage II Ultimate Suspension System with its new Stage III radius arms, and replaces every old suspension component on your pony with new ones that have been designed with maximum articulation and performance in mind.

We were lucky enough to get our hands on a kit to give you an idea at what the system is capable of. We took the new parts and our old Bronco down to Off Road Unlimited (ORU) to install the system. We found the installation time-consuming, but not technically difficult.

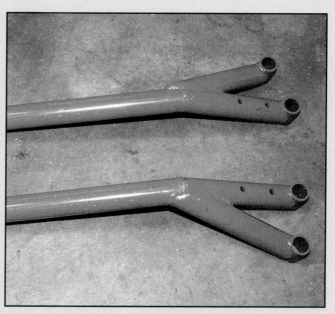

We were so excited about the new radius arms that we had to put them on first. They are 11 inches longer than the stock arms and are ultra-stout with a 3⁄8-inch-thick wall. The aft end has a solid rod that has been machined to accept a giant rod end. Ours were prototypes (as was the rest of the kit) that were cut and welded to make the bend for tire clearance. Future arms will be bent with a heavy-duty bender, eliminating the cut and weld process.

Here is the stock front suspension before surgery. The main travel-limiting factors are the puny shocks, old-school coils, and short radius arms. The Duff kit changes all this.

With a deadline looming, we only had time for a quick trail run, but the increase in articulation and suspension performance was amazing. Of course, this newfound suspension flex also transformed our Bronco into an extremely capable trail rig. It walked through sections that were previously impassable. The Bronco was very stable when crossed up, which we attribute to its equal amounts of articulation front and rear. A quick run up a 23-degree RTI ramp also confirmed the extra flexiness of the suspension. In stock form, the Bronco managed only a pathetic 380, but with the new James Duff system it ramped a very respectable 900 with the same wheels and tires. We suspect the Bronco will easily do 1,100 as our original tire and wheel package rubbed the new shock hoops because of wheels with 4 inches of backspacing.

Equally as impressive was on-road handling, where the Bronco could be driven with confidence and ease. This is in stark contrast to other high-travel trail rigs we have driven on-road, which usually have loads of body roll and spooky steering habits. If you are looking for an easy-to-install suspension for your Bronco—one that gives loads of articulation and can still easily be driven on the highway—then this is it!

The new radius arms are actually a two-piece design with the arms sliding into a head unit that attaches to the axle with C-bushings. By using two bushings at the front of the radius arms, the two-piece design helps to eliminate some of the binding of the stock radius arms during articulation, thus giving extra flex.

The original factory piece is used to attach the head unit to the axle. We also opted to replace all of our wasted bushings with new polyurethane units from James Duff.

The rears of the radius arms attach to the frame using a beefy mount and massive rod end that allows for even more flex. We chose to weld the mounts to save time, but they can be bolted to the frame.

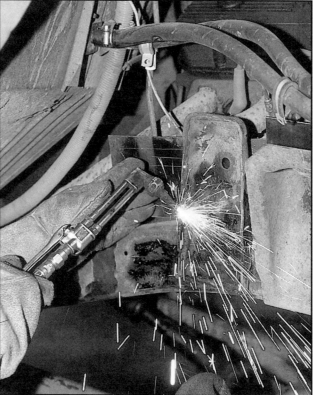

To make room for the James Duff Stage II shock hoops, the old factory shock mounts have to come off. We found the best technique was to use a torch, but a grinder can be used.

Next to go on are the Stage II shock hoops that allow for a much longer shock to be used. Again, we busted out the welder, but they can be bolted on. The inner fenderwells fell out of our Bronco a long time ago, but the Duff hoops are said to fit inside factory fenderwells with a 2-inch body lift. Without the body lift, you'll need to do some sheetmetal trimming.

Our original 3-inch lift coils were replaced with new ones from James Duff. The new coils supply 3 1/2 inches of lift, but are also taller than the originals because they are softer and flexier.

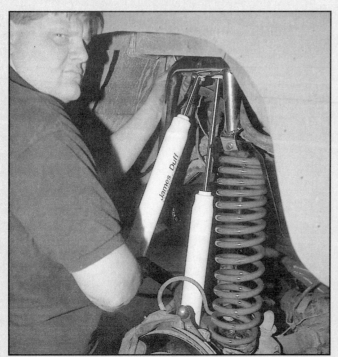

We were even able to coax ORU assistant manager Steve Deitsch out of his air-conditioned office to give us a hand putting shocks on, and he was more than happy to help. The front uses two super-long, 15-inch-travel James Duff 70/30 Auto Adjust shocks per corner to give a massive increase in articulation.

A track bar drop bracket is a necessity. The James Duff bracket bolts onto the original bracket so it is a good idea to check the condition of the original. Ours needed a few welds and we then added a small bead to the sides and top of the new bracket for safety.

Once we finished the front, we shifted our attention to the rear of the Bronco. Short shocks and a bad traction bar design seriously limited articulation out back.

The first pieces to go on the back were the new upper shock mounts. Our Bronco already had a 2-inch body lift so only slight trimming of the body seam was necessary. Once again we welded the piece, but it can bolt on.

To finish off the rear, we used 11-leaf, 3 1/2-inch lift springs from James Duff, which are made to give lots of articulation and handle some extra weight. In this finished shot, you can also see how the 12-inch-travel 70/30 Auto Adjust shocks are positioned. The only pieces that actually need to be welded on are the lower shock mounts.

On our first test-drive of the Bronco we experienced some bumpsteer. A dropped Pitman arm solved this problem. James Duff doesn't include them in the kits because of so many variations (power steering conversions, tie-rod over conversions, and so on), but an easy way to tell if you need one is if your track bar isn't parallel with your drag link.

The last step was to install a set of new James Duff Urethane fender flares. Our original ones were hard fiberglass units that were destroyed from trail usage. The urethane units are flexible and will take more of a beating. We suspect with this much backspacing and articulation that we might have to trim the rear fenders all the way up to body line.

Solving Wheel and Tire Dilemmas

Finding wheels and tires for our Bronco turned out to present quite a dilemma. An eight-lug Dana 60 had been swapped into the rear of our rig some time ago and the front Dana 44 was upgraded to eight-lug, 3⁄4-ton Ford gear to match the rear. Part of the 3⁄4-ton gear included massive dual-piston Ford calipers that only 16.5- or 16-inch wheels would clear (or so we thought). Since 16.5-inch wheels have no safety bead and easily blow beads when aired down, we searched for 16-inch wheels to clear the calipers. However, we quickly discovered that tire choices are still limited for 16-inch wheels. Next, we toyed with the loathsome idea of swapping out to a smaller caliper. Luckily for us, 4 Wheel Parts Wholesalers came to the rescue when it informed us that it makes 15x10-inch, eight-lug Rock Crawlers with a 2 1⁄2-inch backspacing. When bolted on, the Rock Crawlers had enough backspacing to clear our large calipers and rotors. The 15-inch wheels also gave us the opportunity to run 35x12.50R15 Pro Comp Mud Terrains. We have heard good things about these tires and were eager to try them out.

Before . . .

. . . and after.

18 Long-Arm Tactics

We Install and Test Extended Radius Arms for Late '70s Fords

By Alan Huber
Photography by Alan Huber

We just weren't convinced that our '79 Bronco's front suspension was performing up to its true potential. We had already bolted on a set of the softest 4-inch coils we could find, which made the truck ride well enough on the pavement, but off-road, articulation was still lacking. Even with the shock absorbers removed, the axle would bind as it drooped and compressed. Was it the springs or the short factory radius arms restricting axle movement?

We decided to try some new arms since we had seen them work well on early Broncos, but we didn't know if anyone made a set for fullsize '78–'79 Broncos ('73–'79 1/2-ton Ford pickups share the same suspension setup). Some Web surfing for used parts at Jeff's Bronco Graveyard brought us a surprise. There, in the glowing phosphors, was a complete extended radius arm kit developed by Fabritech expressly for mid-to-late '70s fullsize Ford Broncos.

4x4s. Sweet!

The fact the kit was also a bolt-on was way cool since not only is this truck a daily driver and can't be left torn down for more than a weekend at a time, but we weld worse than you can figure skate. Plus, the kit could be installed for this story and its performance evaluated without changing anything else on the truck.

So read forth and prosper.

Radius Arm Anatomy

We're jealous of all the cool suspension parts available for the first generation ('66–'77) Broncos. Extended radius arms, progressive-wound coil springs, multiple-shock systems, and other modern-engineered parts abound for the small Broncos—even though it took Ford seven years of building early Broncos to equal the two-year total of '78–'79 Bronco production. Add in the similar '73–'79 1/2-ton pickups and this becomes a huge market. Thanks to Jeff's Bronco Graveyard (JBG) and Fabritech, the extended-radius-arms-for-fullsize-Fords niche has been filled.

But enough preaching to the choir; it's time to go from the pulpit to the chalkboard. Ford did a great job when it developed the coil-sprung, radius-armed, straight-axled frontend for its trucks. While the design works well enough at stock ride height, bad things happen when it's lifted. Unlike a leaf-sprung vehicle, the Ford design rotates the axle forward (the pinion comes up) significantly as the truck is lifted. Not only is caster lost (approximately 1.2 degrees for each inch of lift), but the arm bushings start to bind in the rear frame bracket, and the coils begin to arc forward on their now-tilted seats.

Most lift kits correct the caster and bracket-bind problems by using a combination of C-bushings (at the axle end of the arm) and drop brackets (each 1 inch of drop restores 1.8 degrees of caster) to lower the rear of the arm, respectively, but little is done to straighten the bowed springs. The JBG/Fabritech radius arms utilize a built-in caster correction of 5 degrees and a slight bracket drop in combination with a tapered block to keep the coils sitting flat. The additional 12 inches of arm length create extra leverage that allows the axle to twist and articulate to a greater degree. Basically, everything is freed up to move easier.

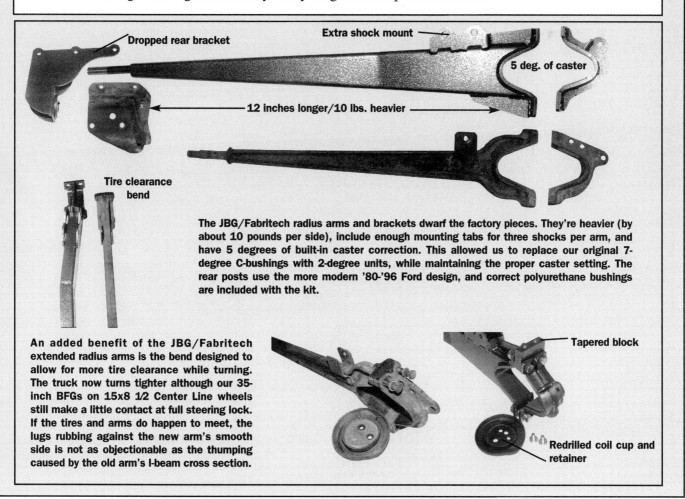

The JBG/Fabritech radius arms and brackets dwarf the factory pieces. They're heavier (by about 10 pounds per side), include enough mounting tabs for three shocks per arm, and have 5 degrees of built-in caster correction. This allowed us to replace our original 7-degree C-bushings with 2-degree units, while maintaining the proper caster setting. The rear posts use the more modern '80-'96 Ford design, and correct polyurethane bushings are included with the kit.

An added benefit of the JBG/Fabritech extended radius arms is the bend designed to allow for more tire clearance while turning. The truck now turns tighter although our 35-inch BFGs on 15x8 1/2 Center Line wheels still make a little contact at full steering lock. If the tires and arms do happen to meet, the lugs rubbing against the new arm's smooth side is not as objectionable as the thumping caused by the old arm's I-beam cross section.

The truck must be safely supported by its frame so the axle will droop to its lowest position. You'll need extra-tall jackstands (at least 24 inches minimum) placed on the front crossmember. Don't put them on the framerails behind the old frame brackets (d'oh!) since you'll need room to drill holes and bolt on the new rear brackets.

While supporting the axle with a floor jack or a second pair of jackstands, remove the front tires and disconnect all of the lower shock mounts and the lower coil spring mounting cup. We were able to leave the track bar attached which helped keep the axle approximately positioned in the vehicle. The front driveshaft, however, had to be unbolted to allow the axle to swing forward far enough to clear the radius arms. With this stuff unattached, use the jack to lower the axle a bit more and you can then remove the radius arm retainer bolts. A good soaking with rust penetrant and a 1/2-inch impact wrench really help to coerce these things apart.

Next, remove the 1 1/8-inch nut from the rear arm mount and take off the old rear frame brackets. Ford used these brackets not only to hold the radius arms, but also to tie in with the tranny mount. The JGB/Fabritech kit includes brackets that bolt on using the factory holes to maintain the stock structural rigidity. All of the kit hardware was top notch, consisting of Grade 8, fine-thread fasteners with washers and nylon lock nuts. Note that the rearmost hole on the side of the frame (arrow) will be used to locate the new frame brackets in the next step.

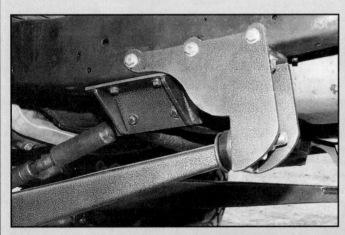

Here's the drill: Make sure you have some sharp drill bits and a good 1/2-inch drill motor since you'll need to hog out eight 1/2-inch holes through the hardened steel of the frame to mount the rear brackets. Pressure is your friend, so your chest will become intimately acquainted with (if not permanently attached to) the handle of your drill. Bolt the JBG/Fabritech frame brackets on, slip the rear of the new arms through the bushings and brackets, and then loosely thread on the supplied palm-sized lock nut. (You'll need a fist-sized 1 5/16-inch socket when this nut gets snugged down later, so be prepared.)

More drilling. At least this part can be done on a drill press if you're so equipped. We aren't. The JBG/Fabritech kit has tapered blocks that install between the radius arms and arm retainers (the block's short side should face the rear of the vehicle) to keep the coils sitting flat. The coil cups and coil retainers must be redrilled at 90 degrees to the factory holes in order to bolt back in proper relationship to the springs. Center the blocks on the bottom of the cups and scribe an outline. Measure 1 inch in from each end along the centerline and drill two 9/16-inch holes. Then transfer these holes to the coil retainers and drill to match. Now you're ready to slap in the C-bushings, making sure they are oriented correctly (they're marked), and bolt everything back together.

Before

After

You're going to need longer shocks, period. The new arms really free up the suspension: our travel (as measured at the shock mount behind the axle) went from 5 3⁄4 inches to 10 inches! The ramp showed the Bronco's suspension twist improved by 23 percent. By using a little right-triangle geometry (sine of angle x hypotenuse = opposite side) we found that the Bronco could drive a tire over a boulder 29 inches tall in the middle of a flat road. Too many numbers? Probably. But all this math hints at what we found out on the trail—namely, the truck now keeps all four wheels planted on the ground much more easily in twisted up sections than with the T-Rex-length factory arms.

Ramp Results

The reasoning behind this story was to see if a simple, bolt-on set of extended radius arms really could improve the suspension performance of an almost-stock, barely-lifted (4 inches) fullsize Ford. While ramp testing isn't the final word on off-road aplomb, it does give some insight into the potential of a certain vehicle. Nothing can replace an experienced driver. The ramp travel index (RTI) indicates how far a vehicle can drive one wheel up a ramp before one of the other three tires begins to lift. This measurement (taken from the centerline of the wheel on, and perpendicular to, the ramp) is divided by the vehicle's wheelbase and multiplied by 1,000 for the final value. We unhooked all the shocks, since many times they are the limiting factor. We also ran all four tires up the ramp and took an average to negate discrepancies in measuring and/or side-to-side performance. See the chart for the results of our wrenching.

Nowadays every cure seems to have a side effect. With the JBG/Fabritech arms we gained an unexpected lift of about 1 1⁄2 inches to the front of the Bronco due to the height of the tapered blocks where the springs sit. Some people may not need or want this extra altitude but it was fine with us since it gave us a total lift of almost 6 inches with only 4-inch springs. To level the truck, we used a set of 1 1⁄2-inch blocks in the rear. Just thought you'd like to know our long-arm tactics.

Ramping Up*

	Stock	Modified
Avg. Ramp Distance (in)	60	74
RTI	573	707

* Ramp was set at 23 degrees and tire pressure was at 30 psi for both tests.

The '78-'79 Bronco wheelbase is 104.7 inches. This Bronco's ramp performance increased 23 percent.

19

Titanic Lift
How to Install the Pro Comp 6-inch Excursion Lift Kit

By Wendy Frazier
Photography by Wendy Frazier

In 1999, Michael Jordan retired from basketball, Wayne Gretzky from hockey, and Ford introduced the 2000 Excursion. While all the comings and goings of people and products were being noted, several companies were working, thankfully, on designing a lift for the big boy Excursion and Super Duty trucks.

One of these companies, Explorer ProComp, now boasts a new 6-incher that renovates the Brady Bunch stock Excursion into something closer to Xena Warrior Princess—minus the princess—that allows you to stuff a set of 35s under it. We went to our local 4 Wheel Parts Performance Center in Burbank, where they were installing the new 6-inch lift on the biggest of the big—the Excursion. The same kit is available for the Super Duty trucks. However, it only yields 4 inches of lift.

It doesn't need to be said, but installing any suspension product is easier with a hydraulic lift. Most of us don't own a hydraulic lift so...make sure to park your vehicle on a flat, hard surface. Stabilize the vehicle by blocking the rear tires and setting the parking brake. Inspect the kit to ensure that it is complete. Start by removing the driver-side track rod bolt at the frame mount, then raise the front of the vehicle and support the frame with jackstands behind the front springs. Check out the rest of the install as we "raise the Titanic."

Support the front axle with a floor or transmission jack and remove the shocks and the stock upper shock mounts. Separate the tie rod from the pitman arm and then remove the stock pitman arm with a pitman arm puller. Remove the sway bar links on both sides at the upper mounts. Save the 12mm bolts for the reassembly. Since you're already there, remove the upper sway bar mounts from the inside of the frame and relocate them under the frame as shown. Using the existing holes, bolt the mount down.

While the space around the wheelwells is free of arm-contorting parts, remove the stock bumpstops. Attach the extended heavy-duty bumpstops using the stock hardware.

Before clipping the wheelwell lining, use your hand to feel behind the lining at the mount cut-out. This will ensure that you won't accidentally slice through any hoses. Use a saw to clip a U-shaped line while following the stock hole. It may seem big at first, but this will allow you room to attach the new mount and dual shocks.

Instead of using extended brake lines, you can bend the brake line bracket by using pliers to bend it towards you (away from the frame) about 90 degrees. This will allow more slack in the brake line.

With the axle still supported by a jack, remove the U-bolts. To remove the front springs, remove the rear leaf bolt nut but don't pull the bolt out yet. Move to the front of the spring and remove the front bolt. To access the front leaf bolt you'll have to also remove the A/C brackets. While holding the weighty front part of the leaf in your arm, slide the rear leaf bolt out and remove the springs. To install the new leaf springs, have a buddy hold the leaf while you insert the rear bolt, and then slide the front bolt into place.

Place the U-bolt bracket/bottom shock mount on top of the new leaf pack, then slide the new U-bolts into place. Torque the U-bolt nuts to 100 lb-ft. Tighten the spring bolts to 130 lb-ft for the 18mm bolts, and 115 lb-ft for the 16mm ones. Reattach the A/C bracket that was removed to access the front spring bolt.

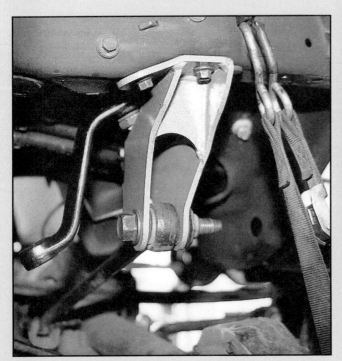

Remove the track rod bracket from the frame. Bolt the ProComp bracket on and reattach the track rod. Install the new pitman arm and tighten the nut down. Reattach the tie rod to the pitman arm and then connect the sway bar.

A friendly tap from a hammer and a hard surface will help you install the shock sleeves into their bushings. Stretch the shocks out and apply the boots. Attach the shocks with the stock hardware and snug 'em down.

In the rear, remove the bottom shock bolts from both shocks. The top shock mount is way up the frame and you can unbolt the top shock bolt by using a lengthy extension and a swivel socket.

Stabilize the rear axle with a transmission jack (or floor jack). Cut the pack clamps off with a grinder as shown (or you can use a hacksaw), and then remove the U-bolts. Measure the add-a-leaf by holding it up to the pack. Decide where the leaf would fit in the progression of the pack. In the Excursion application, we found that it would best fit as the leaf third from the top.

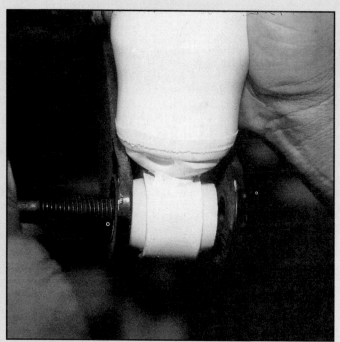

Clamp the leaf pack with a C-clamp. Pull off just the part of the pack that you will be working with. In this application it is the bottom four leaves.

Spray some WD-40 into the bushings, then tap in the metal sleeves. Bolt in the top bolts, then the bottom bolts. Install the wheels and tires and give it a good testdrive. Have the rig aligned, and remember to retighten all hardware after the first 100 miles.

Thread the new center bolt through the bottom four leaves. Paint a few strokes of lithium grease on the top of the ends of the new leaf. Insert the add-a-leaf by sliding the center bolt through the leaf. Using the jack to aid yourself in raising the pack, line up the center bolt with the hole in the top two leaves. Tighten the leaf center bolt all the way.

Because of the variation of factory rear lifts, the Pro Comp kit uses a 1-inch block in conjunction with the stock block and add-a-leaf, depending on what is needed. A replacement leaf pack will soon be available, which is good since we frown on slacking blocks. However, you'll have to front the extra money for the option. Slip the new U-bolts over the axletube along their mounts and torque the U-bolt nuts to 115 lb-ft. The brake lines may become taut and need a little more stretch. Using pliers, bend the brake line bracket towards you about 90 degrees.

Install Tips

• Use a bungee cord (A) to strap up the tie rod to the axle. When you start disconnecting the various rods and bars you'll look up and realize that the octopus-like rods are everywhere. Keep them safely together with a bungee cord.

• Factory spring bolts are secured with Loctite, which makes removal difficult. If you warm the nut with a propane torch to approximately 300 degrees Fahrenheit, the Loctite will release and the hardware can be removed with handtools. (As a precaution, have a fire extinguisher ready whenever using open flame near a vehicle.)

• Thread the bolt, washer, and nut assemblies together after removing them. It may seem like a pain, but when you have the entire axle dropped and are reassembling things you can pick up the entire bolt assembly. You'll save time and hassle by not having to look for the matching washer and nut.

• Use WD-40 (B) to ease the metal insert into the shock bushing.

• Use clamping pliers (C) to grab a hold of the center bolt at the bottom of the spring pack. This will not only assist you in holding the center bolt in place, but give you a hand grip on the center bolt.

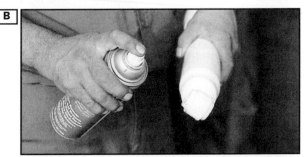

Bump Suckers

Extreme Built and Bolt-On Suspensions

By John Cappa
Photography by *4-Wheel & Off-Road* **Staff**

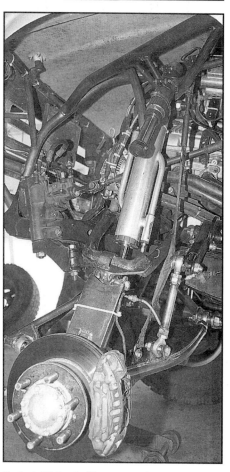

High-speed off-road race parts are in. The technology has slowly been trickling into the 4x4 market. Think we're wrong? Take a look at all the coilover shocks, link suspensions, and tube chassis gobbling up obstacles and blasting across the dunes. These components have been on race trucks for years.

If you're a rockcrawler then there is no arguing that a straight axle is the best. The ability a solid axle has to articulate is far superior to the movement of independent suspension.

For heavy mud, few independent drivelines can withstand more abuse than a straight axle. But if you're more interested in bump-and-jump, then a well-built IFS system may be what you need. More wheel travel is obtainable with independent suspensions, while still keeping the overall vehicle height low for less sway, better maneuverability, and more precise handling. However, don't be fooled by carlike factory independent suspensions. If you try and run your Z71full-blast against

Baja it'll look like one of the cop cars at the Staples Center after a Lakers game. Look for heavy hard parts like what we have here if you want to whump on your wheeler. There are also a few tips for the straight-axle crowd.

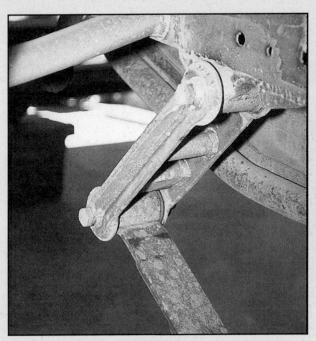

ATS offers long-travel suspensions that include chrome-moly upper and lower A-arms for all IFS Toyota 4x4s including Tundras and Tacomas. The kits offer 12 inches of travel with modified halfshafts.

Straight-axle boys pay attention. Check the length of these shackles found on the rear suspension of the Advanced Toyota Suspensions (ATS) race truck. The leaf springs are way longer than stock and they run underneath the axle. The soft, heavily-arched springs lengthen as they compress. The shackles allow free movement without binding for over 20 inches of vertical wheel travel. Translation—it'll suck bumps.

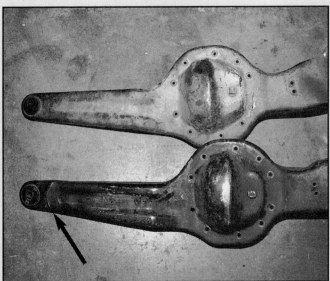

Here's a look at some modified '86-'96 F-150 Twin-Traction Beams (TTB) from Baja Racing Products. The lower beam has been lengthened 1 1/2 inches (arrow). Lengthening the beam increases wheel travel. However, lengthening it more than 1 1/2 inches will cause the differential to hit the driver-side framerail at full bump. The lower ball-joint mounts on both beams have been moved outward. This allows the use of 4-inch coils without using cheesy brackets to drop the beams for proper camber. Modified beams are available for Rangers and Explorers too.

Heavy-duty steering linkages are also available from ATS. Check out the bombproof chrome-moly idler arm. Rod ends and chrome-moly tubing replace toothpick factory tie rods and ends.

Baja Racing Products also has bolt-on long travel arms for '86–'95 Toyota 4x4s. The lift is adjustable from zero to 5 inches with 12 inches of wheel travel. Chrome-moly steering linkages are offered and include spherical rod ends, tie rod tubes, a gussetted steering arm, and a burly idler arm. Custom Porsche 930 CV joints replace the weak factory inner joints and allow full movement of the suspension without binding.

The hot setup on Rangers is to modify the beams for 4-inch coils. F-150 coils (shown) can take more abuse without sagging than the small-diameter Ranger coils. To run F-150 pieces the beams have to be lengthened to pull the coils away from the frame. The factory Ranger coil buckets work with the F-150 coils. Longer radius arms complete the package.

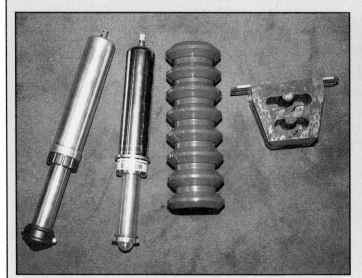

Bumpstops play an important role in the cycling of speed-racer suspensions. We spotted these at Baja Racing Products. On the left are Sway-A-Way and Bilstein air-bumps. They compress up to 4 inches to absorb bottoming-out suspensions. The ribbed cylindrical urethane bumpstop is placed inside a coil spring and provides a progressive stop. The bumpstop on the right is an interlocking urethane piece that is a low-cost alternative to air-bumps.

Off Road Unlimited (ORU) is currently building a sick Suburban that will have a 2000 steel body mounted with Dzus fasteners. The frontend features Dana 60 knuckles mounted on huge A-arms with uniballs instead of ball joints. The centersection is a Dana 60 piece that uses stub shafts for axles. U-jointed halfshafts will transmit power to the wheels.

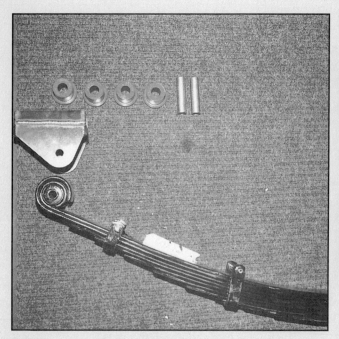

Long-travel leaf springs aren't unheard of. They should be as long as possible, have quite a bit of arc, and have lots of thin leaves. The best way to accommodate these monsters is to mount them under the axle. This 62-inch spring kit from Baja Racing Products offers 19 inches of wheel travel for the rear of a Toyota. The stock Toy springs peter out at about 12 inches of vertical travel.

The best way to make some travel in the rear is with a link-type suspension with coil-overs. The 14-bolt under the Sub at ORU resembles the Stealth Fighter with all the gussetting in place. The axle is located by two long lower links and two V-shaped uppers (not in photo). When set up properly a four-link like this can supply up to 30 inches of jump-sucking wheel travel.

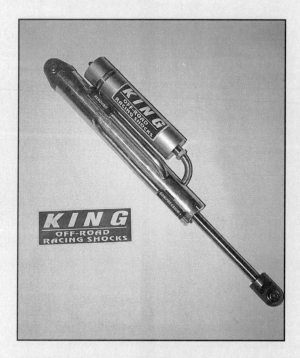

Large diameter shocks are the only way to go. But if you really want to get serious about speed and bumps you'll need to look into a set of bypass shocks like this King. Bypass shocks are position-sensitive rather than velocity. This allows the shocks to be lightly valved for small bumps and stiffer as they come closer to bottoming out.

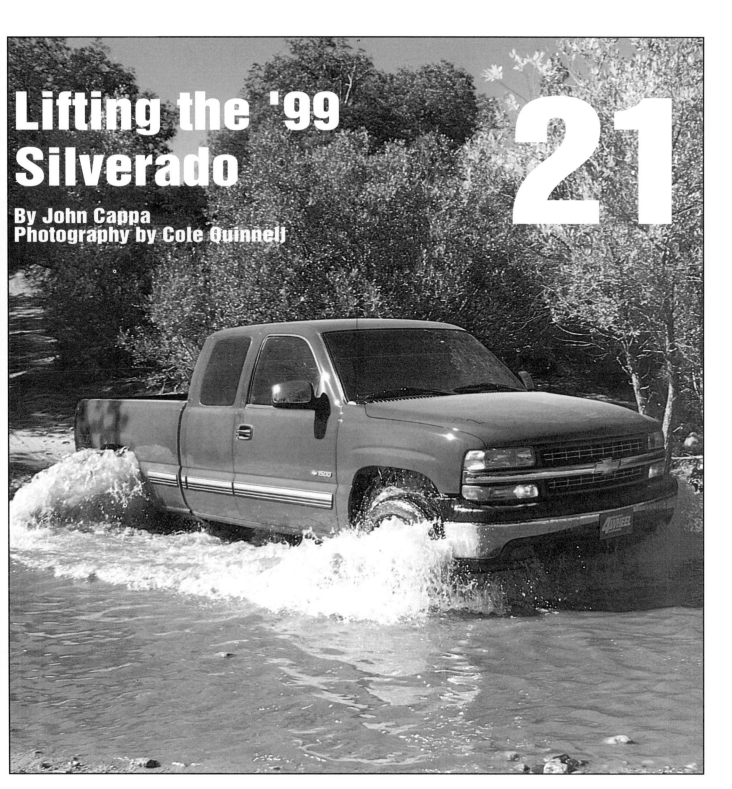

Lifting the '99 Silverado

By John Cappa
Photography by Cole Quinnell

21

When the '99 GM trucks came out with a new suspension and body, it didn't take long for the aftermarket to respond with some super lift kits. Here are some of the best from, Rancho, Superlift, Trail Master, and Tuff Country. There are two 6-inch kits and three 4-inch kits, but each company achieves the lift in a different way. Rather than lead you through the installation of each, we'll point out significant features and focus on the key systems affected such as steering, brakes, and so on.

TUFF COUNTRY

Tuff Country offers a 4-inch and a 6-inch kit for the new GM trucks. The kit is similar in design to the kits for the earlier IFS trucks. The factory control arms are retained by utilizing drop brackets. This method allows the use of factory wheels and tires if desired. Because the kit requires removal of the front crossmember (GM bolted it to one framerail and welded it to the other), Tuff Country offers return-to-stock brackets. To install the 6-inch kit, an exhaust reroute is necessary for driveshaft clearance. Both kits will make an alignment necessary after installation.

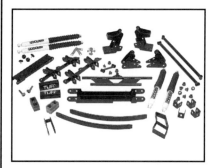

The 6-inch kit includes lateral compression struts (upper right) to help stabilize and strengthen the frontend of the truck. The lift gives enough room for 35-inch tires. The 4-inch kit makes room for 33x12.50s. A CV-type driveshaft is included in 4- and 6-inch kits for trucks equipped with the Autotrac transfer case. Both kits include drop-down brackets to allow the use of the original brake lines.

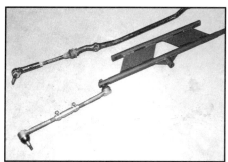

The stock centerlink (top) is replaced with the new drop-down version (bottom). This assures that the steering functions properly without binding or rubbing on other components.

Installation of the upper control-arm drop brackets necessitates the removal (cutting) of the bumpstops. The bracket pictured is installed down and to the right of where it is positioned, and the factory upper arms are bolted to the bracket. The sway bar is also retained. Tuff Country found that by flipping the bar over, the need for longer sway-bar links is eliminated.

TUFF COUNTRY

Amount of lift	4 inches	6 inches
Largest tire that will fit	33x12.50 on 10-inch wheel recommended	33x12.50 35-inch
Alignment after Installation?	Yes	Yes
Reroute exhaust?	No	Yes
Cutting or torching?	Yes, remove front crossmember and bumpstops; trimming for differential clearance also needed	Same as 4-inch kit
Is it reversible?	Yes, bracket kit available	Yes, bracket kit available
Is front diff lowered?	Yes	Yes
Will stock wheels work?	Yes	Yes
Rear lift	4-inch blocks and 2 1/2-inch add-a-leaf; rear springs available	5 1/2-inch blocks & 2 1/2-inch add-a-leaf; rear springs available

SUPERLIFT

The Superlift kit uses brackets to drop the differential and suspension components, similar to the company's kit for the previous-generation Chevy. In the rear, the factory blocks are replaced with 5-inch lift blocks. Plans are also in the works to offer a block/add-a-leaf combination and replacement rear leaf springs. The height gained from the kit will be 5 1/2 to 6 inches over stock. This will provide clearance for 36-inch tires mounted on 16x10 wheels. The stock tire-and-wheel combo will also fit.

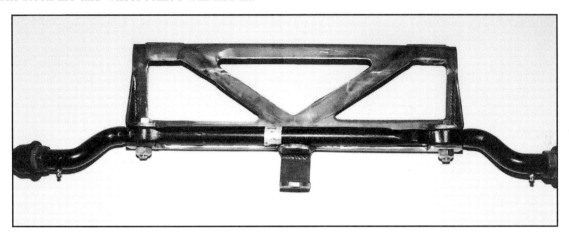

Superlift has a unique approach to steering correction on the '99 GM trucks. The original centerlink is used in conjunction with a gusseted drop bracket and a second idler arm. This design makes replacement of worn parts much simpler because it uses all of the factory steering linkages.

Superlift is working to fit its kit on Autotrac-equipped trucks without replacing the front driveshaft. If they are able to accomplish this, the kit will offer a considerable savings to the customer over kits that require driveshaft replacement. The sway bar and end links are retained. To compensate for the lift, the bar is flipped upside-down. An alignment will be necessary once the kit is installed. The design of the kit ensures that the truck can be aligned to factory spec. As of this writing no exhaust reroute is necessary.

Superlift	
Amount of lift	5 1/2-6 inches
Largest tire that will fit	36-inch on 16x10 wheel
	10-inch wheel recommended
Alignment after installation?	Yes
Reroute exhaust?	No
Cutting or torching?	Yes, bumpstop cups and a small portion of front crossmember need to be removed
Is it reversible?	Yes, minor fabrication required
Is front diff lowered?	Yes
Will stock wheels work?	Yes
Rear lift	5-inch blocks and add-a-leaf combo; rear springs available

The basic kit includes a hoop-style double-shock system for the frontend. Since the truck rides more like a car from the factory, this addition firms up the ride for towing and gives better handling on and off road. Very little cutting is required for the installation of this kit. The bumpstop cups and about 3 inches of the differential crossmember need to be removed. No welding is necessary, but returning the vehicle to stock will require some fabrication (no return-to-stock brackets are available). The kit includes brake-line relocation brackets so the factory rubber lines are maintained.

Rancho

Rancho uses beefy drop brackets that relocate the factory A-arms for a 4-inch lift. This method allows the use of the original tires and wheels if desired, but 34-inch tires will fit. Unlike lifts for the earlier-model GM IFS trucks, this one does not require an exhaust reroute.

This photo shows the complete kit. The factory torsion-bar crossmember is replaced, and the original sway bar is retained but flipped upside-down and uses the original links and hardware. This photo is of a pre-production kit, so be aware that some parts may change. The factory brake lines will be retained by utilizing drop brackets rather than the new lines shown in the photo.

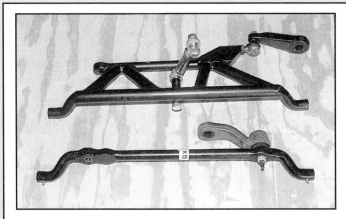

The original centerlink and pitman arm are replaced with Rancho parts that compensate for the lift. A second idler arm consisting of a short link and two rod ends stabilize the centerlink. Rancho recommends an alignment before and after installation of its kit. Doing an alignment before the lift will ensure that your truck's frame and suspension are in good condition.

Installing the kit requires some cutting. The bumpstop brackets and a frame support need to be removed in order for the lift components to be installed. For this installation a plasma cutter was utilized, but a torch or a grinder can be used. The company plans to offer return-to-stock brackets at a later date.

The Silverado has factory 2-inch rear blocks. Instead of stacking blocks, Rancho supplies 5-inch blocks that allow the removal of the stock ones. This gives your truck a level stance. New U-bolts are also installed.

RANCHO

Amount of lift	4 inches
Largest tire that will fit	34-inch
Alignment after installation?	Yes, alignment before and after installation
Reroute exhaust?	No
Cutting or torching?	Yes, factory bumstop mounts and one differential-support bracket
	need to be removed; trimming of upper A-arm mounts is necessary
Is it reversible?	Yes, bracket kit will be made available at a later date
Is front diff lowered?	Yes
Will stock wheels work?	Yes
Rear lift	5-inch blocks

TRAIL MASTER

The kit offered by Trail Master is a bolt-on 4-inch kit with no welding required. However, the original front crossmember needs to be trimmed for clearance before the differential can be lowered. Trail Master assured us that the kit is totally reversible.

Trail Master uses tubular upper control arms with greaseable polyurethane bushings. Ball-joint spacers and new TRW greaseable upper ball joints are also included. Drop brackets are used for the factory lower control arms and differential. This improves wheel travel while maintaining acceptable driveline angles. A replacement centerlink, extended tie-rod sleeves (pictured), and new inner and outer tie-rod ends (not pictured) are included in the kit. The 2-inch blocks are stacked on top of the factory blocks (we don't recommend stacking blocks) and an add-a-leaf is also required to bring up the rear. The kit provides room for up to 34-inch tires and will work with the factory wheels. Trail Master recommends 33-inch tires on 10-inch-wide wheels. Unlike the older GM trucks, the new trucks do not require an exhaust reroute for front driveshaft clearance. If your truck is equipped with an Autotrac transfer case, the kit will still work, but a replacement dual-cardan (CV-type) front driveshaft, available from Trail Master, will need to be installed.

TRAILMASTER

Amount of lift	4 inches
Largest tire that will fit	34-inch
Alignment after installation?	Yes
Reroute exhaust?	No
Cutting or torching?	Yes, trimming of front crossmember is necessary
Is it reversible?	Yes
Is front diff lowered?	Yes
Will stock wheels work?	Yes
Rear lift	52-inch blocks and 2-inch add-a-leaf

Fabtech's Fall Guy Suspension

A 6-Inch Kit for '99-and-Newer Silverado/Sierra Pickups

By David Kennedy
Photography by David Kennedy

22

No, we're not talking about some lame remake of the early '80s stuntman TV show that starred a high-flying 3⁄4-ton GMC pickup (we all know Lee Majors just played a supporting role). We're talking about the newest 6-inch lift on the market for your '99-and-newer Silverado or Sierra 1⁄2-ton truck. We got a sneak peak at this IFS kit when Brent Riley of Fabtech Motorsports in Brea, California, invited us down to its facility to check out some of its newest innovations for these popular trucks.

With its kit, Fabtech has implemented all the latest IFS suspension lift tricks, and introduced more ground clearance and the ability to run stock offset wheels. They even went so far as to offer a whole slew of options to work with the base kit so you can tailor the suspension for your own needs and wallet. We snooped around the Fabtech shop as they bolted on the new Fabtech-blue goodies so we could see for ourselves just what makes this kit so different from all the others on the market.

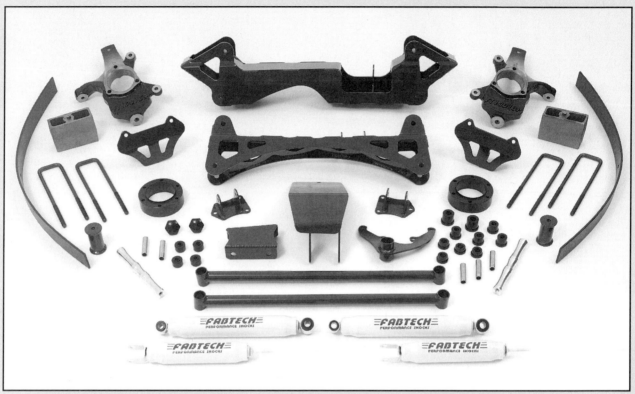

Fabtech's 6-inch lift kit for '99 and-newer GMC Sierra/Chevy Silverados costs about $1,500. It uses 315/75R-16 tires mounted on 16x9-inch wheels with 4 5⁄8-inch backspacing. Total installation time is about 6–7 hours.

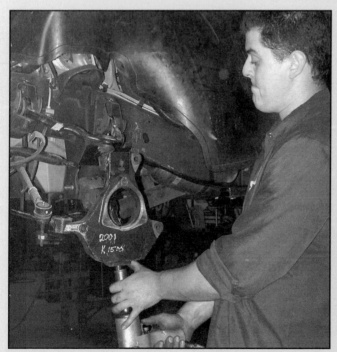

With the front of the truck off the ground, the stock suspension striptease begins by removing everything but the upper A-arms. Mark the torsion bars "left" and "right" before you remove them, and then call a strong buddy to help you take out the front differential assembly.

It's Sawzall city for the front differential—but it's nothing to be afraid of. The stock mount has to be whacked off so that the new Fabtech mount can be added. You'll also have to grind away some of the aluminum fins (arrow) on the pinion support to clear the truck's frame. This allows for proper driveshaft angles for Autotrac-equipped trucks.

Bolt in the rear half of the subframe first so you have a place to bench-press the front differential up to. The subframe pieces are shot-peened (this cleans and stress-relieves the metal) and then powdercoated blue. The mounting ear that you cut off the differential is replaced with a new Fabtech (arrow) mount that bolts into the aluminum housing.

Here we're pointing to where a small L-bracket was cut off the frame to clear the now lowered differential. You'll have to make this cut before you mount any of the new Fabtech parts, or reinstall the front differential. Even with this little trim job it gets tight in here, which is why you have to grind away some of the differential housing too.

When you have the front half of the subframe in place you can mount the optional steering stabilizer (PN FTS8002) while it's still easy to get at. Stick the original lower A-arms into their new homes in the Fabtech subframe, but leave everything finger tight for now.

The two-piece subframe is bolted together with this 1/4-inch-thick skidplate that protects the delicate drivetrain parts without decreasing ground clearance. As a bonus it ties the subframe together for even greater strength.

In the wheelwell, the suspension is starting to take shape with Fabtech's new cast-iron steering knuckles that maintain the factory steering geometry and let you run stock offset wheels. With these new cast knuckles, the factory steering and upper A-arms stay just the way GM designed them, which makes it faster for the installer, easier on the alignment shop, and better for you.

When you bolt in the CV shaft you will need to add these spacers to make up for the new wider front track width. Fabtech supplies you with longer metric bolts and recommends you torque them in a cross pattern.

For maximum dampening and control in the really fast and rough stuff, Fabtech offers a triple shock kit (PN FTS51001) with or without the Fox shocks (PN FTS51004) shown here. The kit consists of a tubular shock hoop and a plate that bolts on to the upper control arm for the lower mount. Regardless of the shock option you choose, new longer Fabtech shocks fit in the stock shock location.

The front suspension upgrade is completed by drilling new holes in the frame and bolting in the torsion bar crossmember drop-down brackets. After the stock torsion bars are set to the factory preload specs, the front suspension is ready to go.

The standard Fabtech 6-inch lift comes with shocks, blocks, and add-a-leaves to bring up the rear. That's cool and all, but we chose to install the optional new rear spring packs (PN FTS41700). While we were at it, we had Fabtech mount up these optional traction bars (PN FTS61001) for the ultimate in axlewrap control.

With the truck riding on a set of 315/75R-16 tires, check out all the new ground clearance you get at static ride height. The skidplate clears a little over 12 inches and the rear crossmember has been contoured with ground clearance as a priority.

23 Explorer Pro Comp Silverado Lift

By David Kennedy
Photography by David Kennedy

As expected, the GM Silverado and GMC Sierra pickups have flooded the light truck market with hundreds of thousands of 1/2-ton 4x4s that need to be lifted. We've met the chief engineer for GM's fullsize truck line, and trust us, he's a smart guy. But until the Silverados come from the factory with 35-inch tires we're still going to have to find ways to lift these trucks. And now that these new K1500s have been around for awhile, Explorer Pro-

Comp has taken the time to research and engineer a bolt-on kit that doesn't use costly new cast-iron spindles. Instead Explorer Pro-Comp has gone with its traditional GM IFS lift design that drops both the upper and lower A-arms 6 inches. The result is a pretty beefy lift kit that costs less than a lot of its competitors.

We headed out to Mesa, Arizona, to see Mike Boyd at Off Road Unlimited when we heard he was going to have

his right-hand man Brett Corder install the new Explorer Pro-Comp 6-inch kit on their shop truck. Brett can install an IFS lift kit in his sleep, or in a driveway, but he says doing it in his sleep is easier. We have been fortunate to get to work with the best off-road shops in the country, and we jumped at the chance to have Boyd and Corder walk us through an install.

1. Corder's secret to lifting an IFS Silverado is to leave much of the suspension in place to save time and eliminate the need to lift heavy suspension components. During the install he always had the upper or lower A-arm, CV-shaft, and calipers bolted in place. The first step in installing a lift is to support the truck on a hoist and remove the torsion bars, shocks, and tie rods so you can unbolt the lower A-Arms from where they pivot in the frame.

2. Every GM lift kit we have ever seen requires you to cut this differential-mounting ear off of the lower crossmember. The Explorer Pro-Comp kit is no different. The instructions call for you to make this cut with the front differential removed from the truck, but Corder finds he can make a more accurate cut by leaving it in place. Again this saves steps and time, and because three other bolts hold in the front differential, there is no need to take it out of the truck.

3. The frame-cutting party continues by removing the factory GM upper bumpstop mounts from both the driver and passenger side (shown) of the truck. The instructions tell you to use a hole saw to cut out the welds that hold these suckers in place, but that takes forever and will ruin the best hole saws. Corder uses a Sawzall to cut it off flush with the frame and then grind down any rough spots.

4. The premise of all IFS GM lift kits over 4 inches is to lower the mounting points for both the upper and lower A-arms. This is always done with some form of new subframe that bolts in where the lower A-arms were mounted from the factory. In the case of this Explorer Pro-Comp kit, the rear piece (of the two-piece) subframe bolts in with the stock lower A-arm bolts and with six new bolts that must have holes drilled where the bumpstop we just cut off were located. The directions provide you with an idea of where the holes will be, but Corder used the new subframe as a template to make sure he got it dead-on.

5. With the rear part of the subframe bolted in place, Corder supported the differential with a screw jack and removed the three bolts that still held it in the stock location. Free of the truck, the front differential was then lowered into the cradle of the new subframe and bolted loosely in place. The CV-shafts, differential vent, and central axle disconnect can all be left in place by doing the install Corder's way.

6. The front half of the subframe was then bolted in place. Pro-Comp has you drill four vertical holes into the truck's frame to support the new subframe. Again, by bolting the subframe into the old lower A-arm mounts, it can be used as a template to locate where the new holes need to be. With both the front and rear subframes in place, Corder then used a prybar and a screw jack to maneuver the lower A-arms into their new mounts, which are now 6 inches closer to the ground—hence the 6-inch lift. Once in place all of the bolts are installed and the nuts are left loose.

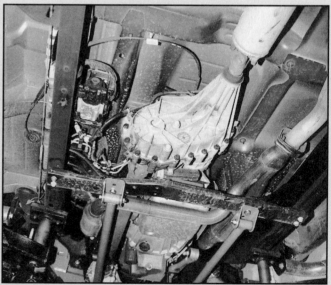

7. GM redesigned the idler arm on the '99-and-up Silverado/Sierra to be stronger and last longer. In order to support the drop-down steering truss that Pro-Comp uses to correct the steering geometry, two new greasable rod end links are incorporated into the front lower subframe. These two links act as additional idler arms and share the stresses exerted by big tires and off-roading on the pitman arm and factory idler arm. It helps to have small hands if you are going to make these modifications to the steering with the front differential in the truck.

8. We don't know who started the trend of adding these anticompression struts to the now 6-inch lower subframe but we'd like to thank them. The Pro-Comp kit uses more bolts and reinforcement brackets than any other kit we've tested to hold the new two-piece lower subframe in place. So if all the bolts stay tight, this should be a strong kit.

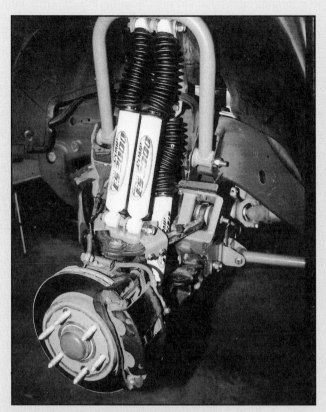

9. The front half of the lift kit is completed with an optional triple-shock kit that is available from Pro-Comp. Notice how the shock hoop bolts in where the stock upper A-arm used to pivot. Also notice that the upper A-arm has been moved down 6 inches to keep them parallel with the lower A-arm. The new rear A-arm mount is actually part of the new lower subframe, while the front mount for the upper A-arm is all new and bolts in place with four bolts. Before installing the torsion bars make sure to route the stock brake lines and ABS wires so they don't get torn as the suspension cycles and the wheels turn.

10. With the Pro-Comp kit, driveshaft vibration problems are suppose to be a thing of the past even with NVG 246 Autotrac transfer case–equipped trucks. Corder reinstalled the factory torsion bars after he relocated the torsion bar crossmember down a few inches with these Pro-Comp mounts. The new mounts index off of rivets in the frame and should be measured, marked, and drilled accurately to ensure the crossmember will bolt back in place.

11. The rear lift uses a combination of add-a-leaves and blocks with new longer ES3000 shocks to get the increase in ride height. Using a screw jack, and doing one side at a time Brett flew through the rear install in about a tenth of the time it took him to do the front.

12. These rear traction bars are available as an option from Explorer Pro-Comp to keep axlewrap down. The bars bolt to the rear axle with a plate that sandwiches between the axletube and the lift block. You have to install the rear of the bar first, and then (with the truck on the ground) mark and drill the new holes for the front mount.

24

RCD's Silverado Lift

By David Kennedy
Photography by David Kennedy

It wasn't long before we got tired of taking our 2000 "Stuckerado" out into the desert only to have to hitch a ride with someone else when we were just starting to have fun. We knew we needed more tire because the 245s weren't cutting it, but we questioned how well the new GM IFS would hold up to the almost 35-inch-tall tires we wanted to run. We were also a little afraid of what would become of our warranty should the 4L80E transmission up and die. But in the end, one too many people mistakingly thought our truck was an El Camino, so we said, "What the hell" and went for it.

Enter Race Car Dynamics with its new 6-inch lift for '99-and-newer K2500s. We had RCD install the new eight-lug kit on our pickup at its top-secret prototype facility in southern California. Plan on being without your truck for at least a day if you have the lift professionally installed, and even longer if you do it yourself.

Now we admit we got a little too excited and went with some steamroller tires for floating over the sand. We had a set of 315/75R16 Pro-Comp All Terrains mounted on Weld Racing 16x8 Velocity wheels. If you want the front suspension to be able to

move, learn from our mistakes and go with a 305/75R16 because right now our tires rub just pulling out of the driveway. The truck rides great and the All Terrain tread is easy to live with. Now the truck floats down the road, yet it can still be pushed hard through the corners thanks to the massive grip of the 315s. Yes, power is down compared to stock but we can still spin the tires if the Gov-Loc doesn't kick in. We plan to swap the 3.73s for some 4.56s, but that means ripping out the front axle again.

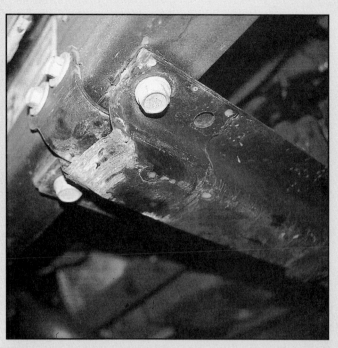

There are surprisingly few parts in this 6-inch IFS lift for our K2500 Silverado, but that is a good thing! Fewer parts mean fewer bolts to come loose and a stiffer suspension foundation to build on. RCD's kit uses a two-piece lower subframe powdercoated "Gator Black" to achieve the 6 inches of lift, and Bilstein shocks are used exclusively to dampen the bumps.

This is why we needed the lift. It doesn't matter what type of front suspension you have when the transmission crossmember is the lowest point of the truck. We bashed it pretty good on a few rocks while listening to "Like a Rock" on the way to the trailhead. Our Chevy had major ground clearance issues, and with 245/75R16 tires we are just happy the rocker panel didn't get whacked too.

RCD's kit differs from other IFS lift kits in that the upper A-arm is left undisturbed in the factory location. Here the technicians remove the stock steering knuckle from the upper ball joint by hitting the knuckle with two hammers. This method is preferred by many mechanics as it doesn't require any special tools and won't damage the joints.

The new RCD knuckle (right) is every bit as strong as the factory casting (left), and has been designed with raised mounting pads for the tie rods and upper ball joints. These revised mounting locations let you keep all the factory steering parts, and eliminate the need for brackets to move the upper control arm. The guy at the alignment shop will love you for that because all the adjustments are made with the stock hardware.

You still have to break out the Sawzall to cut this part of the lower frame in order to remove the front differential. With the lift installed, the aluminum housing of the differential will need to fit here. RCD's kit provides you with a steel plate to weld in and box the section that you have cut. Make sure your installer doesn't skip that part!

Break out the grease gun and lube it, but otherwise leave the steering alone because it's fine as is. RCD told us that up until August 2000, 3/4-ton trucks used 1/2-ton tie rod ends. So check your build date (on the driver-side door) and take comfort in knowing that you can upgrade to the bigger 2500HD tie rods by having the steering knuckles drilled for them if you want. We also found out that our truck has the frame mount for a factory steering stabilizer, but the corresponding hole in the centerlink is not drilled like it is on 2500HDs. Robbed again!

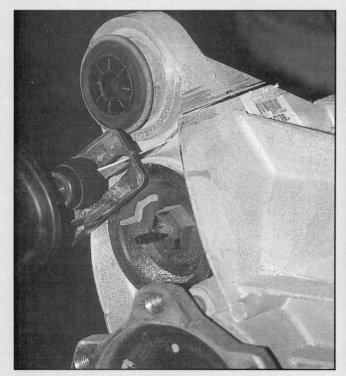

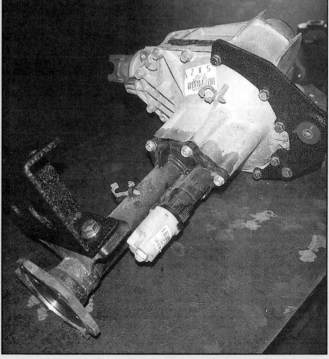

This is the AAM 9 1/4-inch ring gear front axle from our truck with RCD's new differential mount bolted into the aluminum housing. You must cut off the stock mount (left) without cutting into the differential vent. Our K2500 has a cast-iron passenger-side axletube (where the RCD drop down bracket is bolted), while K1500s use cast iron or aluminum.

With the front axle back in the truck, driveshaft clearances can be checked. Depending on the engine combination the exhaust may need to be dimpled. We were lucky and didn't have any clearance problems with the 2 1/2-inch down pipe on our 6.0L.

The RCD kit requires no driveshaft modifications even if you have an Autotrac-equipped (NVG 263) truck. The RCD kit lowers the front differential 4 inches and rotates the pinion angle up toward the transfer case slightly. Our truck uses the NVG 261 transfer case that has a conventional floor shifter and it hasn't rattled us with any driveline vibrations.

Completely assembled with Bilstein shocks, the new front suspension rides and functions better than stock. Track width is increased by about an inch, and if the torsion bars are cranked to their stock pre-load, the truck will ride as soft as it did before the lift.

Longer Bilstein shocks and 4-inch blocks work with stock rear springs to keep all the weight capacities of a 3/4-ton truck. A Mag-Hytec differential cover was added to keep the baby 14-bolt Gov-Loc–equipped axle alive when romping through the sand and snow. We'll have to find another place to mount the 315 spare because it will interfere with the rear axle if you try to mount it under the bed.

Pro Comp's new 315/75R16 (35x12.5x16) All Terrains have a "D" load range rating and were mounted on a set of Weld Racing's new Velocity wheels. These wheels are part of the new EVO line of one-piece cold forged aluminum wheels and have a 3,500-pound weight capacity. Lightweight wheels and tires will keep the IFS alive. With that in mind our new wheel and tire combo weighs just slightly more than the factory stuff. Our 315s rubbed on the front air dam until we attacked it with a razor blade. Unfortunately they still rub on the front bumper and rear inner wheelwell if you flex the suspension more than halfway. We could crank the torsion bars up to their max, but the tires would still rub.

For those of you who think the new 2500HDs are still too low, the same RCD will work for you too. This Duramax-equipped '01 Crew Cab was fitted with the RCD 6-inch kit after the steering knuckles were reamed for the larger tie rod ends, and the rear lower subframe was trimmed to clear the larger aluminum casting around the pinion gear.

Tuff Country Suburban

25

By David Kennedy
Photography by David Kennedy and Christian Hazel

A Suburban is a lot of truck to take out onto the trail, but that doesn't mean you have to settle for rolling around on stock tires. Most of the places we like to go on the weekends were tearing at our front air dam and reaching for our running boards. The low ride height (not our wife) was the limiting factor in where we could take the family four-wheeling.

So when Tuff Country introduced its new 4-inch lift for 2000-and-newer Suburbans and Tahoes we had to check it out. Tuff Country's kit is designed for trucks that have the new five-link rear suspension and retains the Autoride system. GM engineers spent a lot of time and money developing the Autoride system (91 pages of the factory service manual are devoted to "Real Time Dampening"). Tuff Country recommends a certified mechanic perform the installation, so we packed up our stuff and headed to PG Series' new Hard Rock Cafe–like facility in El Cajon, California, to have the lift installed.

Our Suburban was already up on the lift when we got to PG Series, so we began snapping photos as the torsion bars and some dried mud were unloaded and removed. The Tuff Country kit supplies brackets that lower this crossmember to compensate for the relocation of the front A-arms. They give no provisions to reattach the mud, but we're sure you can figure that one out on your own.

There are as many wires and hoses holding the front suspension on this truck as there are bolts, so disconnect the wheel speed sensors, shock load sensors, ride height sensors, and the front calipers before you pull the trigger on that air gun. The front A-arm suspension should be removed as an assembly and placed out of harm's way while you strip the rest of the truck.

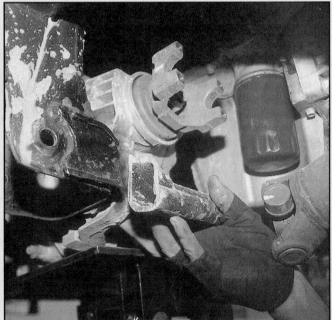

The entire front suspension and drivetrain must be removed prior to installing the Tuff Country kit. The factory aluminum skidplate comes off and the lower suspension crossmember is unbolted and discarded. The driveshaft is then unbolted and the front differential is prepared for removal by disconnecting the vent tube and front axle actuator switch.

About 6 inches of this L-shaped bracket must be cut off in order to facilitate lowering the front differential. This cut is nothing to be afraid of, and the instructions provide you with a clear illustration of where to make the cut. If you think you might return the vehicle to stock at a later time, this piece can be welded back on.

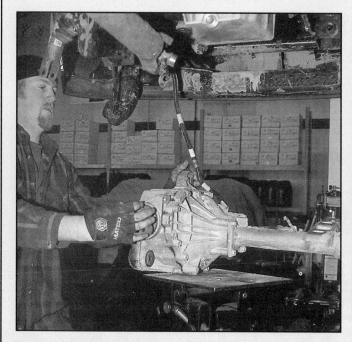

The front differential was supported on a transmission jack and lowered out of the truck after unbolting it from the top three mounting points. That electrical connector is for the front axle disconnect that we advised you to remove in the previous step. We forgot, and were lucky to find there is enough slack in the wire to not damage the actuator. You may not be so lucky.

With the suspension and front axle mess out of the way, you can move on to the steering. A dropped centerlink is used in conjunction with your stock tie rods to regain the factory steering geometry. An additional idler arm is added to the new centerlink to support the extra load of larger tires and off-road use.

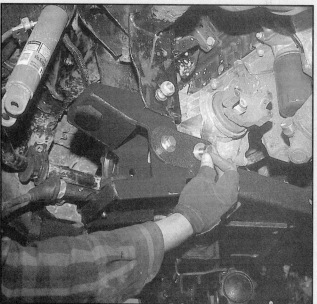

Time to fire up the torch because you have to cut off most of the original suspension's attachment points from the frame. Again the kit's instructions outline where the cuts have to be made, but take your time, as you don't want to cut any more than you have to. Take care not to get the torch too close to the factory shocks, as high heat will damage them. We'd recommend removing them before making your cuts.

If you liked building things with your Erector set as a child, you will love putting this lift together. The kit uses 17 laser-cut, 1/4-inch-thick steel plates to lower the front differential and A-arms. There are a lot of bolts here, so make sure to use the hardware specified by the instructions and use Loctite to keep it all from coming loose. We called the tech line, and Tuff Country requires you to retorque all fasteners after the first 1,000 miles and then every 3,000 miles thereafter.

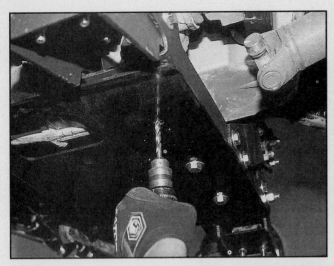

The kit comes with a two-piece skidplate that is much beefier than the stock piece. It bolted into the new lower crossmember and required a little massaging with the drill to get all of the bolt holes to line up. The skidplate looks like it will take a beating without complaint, and adds strength to the new suspension.

The upper and lower A-arms are bolted into their new locations on the Tuff Country brackets. The upper arms are attached with new bolts (shown here being tapped into position) that have a built-in cam to make alignment adjustments easy. The instructions recommend that the alignment be checked every six months after the kit is installed to ensure proper steering and tire wear.

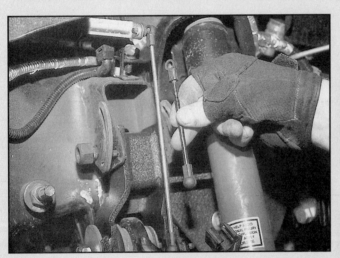

The beauty of this kit is that it allows you to retain all the comfort and performance of GM's Autoride suspension by effectively adapting the factory shocks to work with the 4-inch lift. Factory suspension position sensors are retained by using longer rods to compensate for the lift.

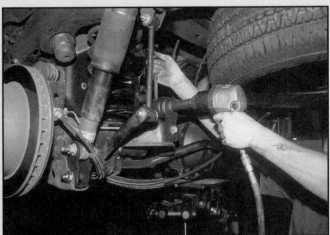

GM is really trying to make these 1/2-ton trucks ride like cars, so new for 2000 is a five-link coil-sprung rear suspension. Tuff Country hasn't missed a step, and rear lift height is achieved with coil-spring spacers that are screwed into the upper spring towers. Additional bracketry is bolted on to keep the stock rear shocks and track bar in place. New longer sway bar links are also provided.

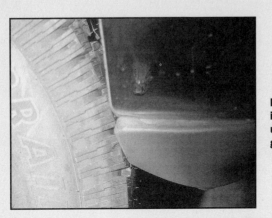

If you want to mount 315/75R16 tires on 16x8 wheels like we did, then 4 inches of lift won't be enough. PG Series cranked the torsion bars all the way up and did some air dam trimming to get the tires to clear, but don't expect to get much travel out of the suspension without massive tire rub.

Raising Your Ramcharger

By Christian Hazel
Photography by John Cappa and Christian Hazel

Yes, you can have fun in a stock 4x4, but not much. Dragging bumpers, knocking rocker panels, and rubbing tires start to suck eggs after about four minutes. And then there's that look that screams "weenie!" Adding a lift allows you to fit bigger tires, improves your approach and departure angles, and gives you that bad-ass, take-no-prisoners look that makes you feel cooler than Governor Jesse Ventura in a pink feather boa.

We were tired of the station-wagon-with-a-front-axle look of our '85 Ramcharger and wanted to install a new suspension that would not only allow us to run bigger tires, but would improve the ride and flex over our stock 220,000-mile suspension. We chose to go with a 6-inch Skyjacker system with new front and rear springs and decided to install it ourselves in our driveway. However, as we describe in the sidebar "Do It Yourself?," there's probably no way you'll be able to get every bolt out of an older vehicle. While the Skyjacker suspension went on easily, the old suspension fought us tooth and nail. Chances are you'll need a little help.

Since 6 inches is a pretty large jump over stock, a lot of things need addressing. Our application required a raised steering arm, lengthened brake lines front and rear, 3-inch sway bar drop brackets, and an adjustable drag link to center the steering wheel and allow for an equal turning radius. Also, since the Skyjacker springs are very soft and flexy, the stock front driveshaft kept separating. We called Six States and gave our measurements. The company sent us a long-travel front driveshaft with a Saginaw CV that matched our stock setup at the transfer case, and a 1310 U-joint at the front Dana 44. The stock rear driveshaft fit, but it vibrated badly at speeds over 60 mph, so we had Six States ship us a spankin' new rear shaft with a 1330 CV joint at the transfer case and a 1310 U-joint at the rear Dana 60. Six States also supplied us with new yolks for both

1. A trip through the Skyjacker catalog got us everything we'd need to lift our Dodge 6 inches. The system includes front and rear springs, shocks, bushings, U-bolts, and hardware. We also ordered Skyjacker's slick extended braided steel brake lines, a raised steering arm, an adjustable drag link, and 3-inch sway bar drop brackets.

differentials and the rear of the transfer case.

Yokohama has come out with a 315/75/16-sized Geolandar MT that we've been dying to try. The metric size is equivalent to a 35x12.5-inch tire and offers a big-rubber option to those not wanting to grind their calipers for 15-inch wheels. We had Stockton Wheels make us some 16x8-inch wheels with seven-hole vented centers and 4-inch backspacing. The combo not only looks killer, but it grips and grabs anything you put in its path.

Since just about everyone knows by now how to lift a leaf-sprung vehicle, we'll skip the blow-by and focus more on some of the problems we encountered during our install. Just remember to lube the poly bushings, don't tighten any of the spring-eye or U-bolts until the vehicle is sitting on the ground under it's own weight, and retorque all of the bolts after the first 100 miles or so.

2. We started the installation three days earlier by soaking every nut, bolt, and fitting with penetrating lube. It didn't help much. With jackstands under the frame and front axle, we removed the wheels and tires, U-bolts, shocks, and spring-eye bolts. We needed a drift and hammer, but the bolts eventually came out.

3. Bummer. The passenger-side shackle hit the exhaust pipe and wouldn't come off. Since the exhaust bolts were rusty beyond belief, removing the pipe wasn't an option. Instead, we used a bottle jack to raise the pipe enough to get the shackle off. Butch!

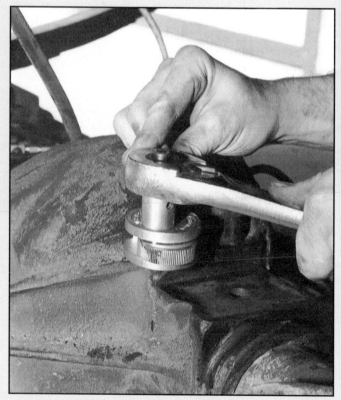

4. Dodge had to be different and used studs instead of U-bolts at the pumpkin that are too short for the five-leaf Skyjacker front spring packs. You could try double-nutting the studs to remove them, but we used a Craftsman stud remover to keep the profanity to a minimum.

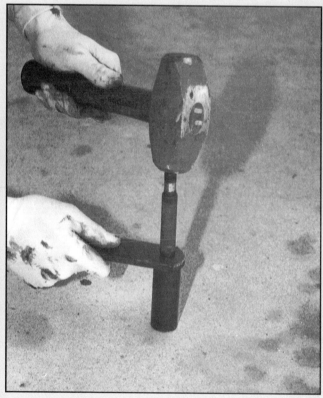

5. Our stock shackle bushing sleeves had fused to the bolts (above, top). Rather than messing with them, we knocked out the stock bolts and replaced them with 1/2-inch Grade 8 hardware (above).

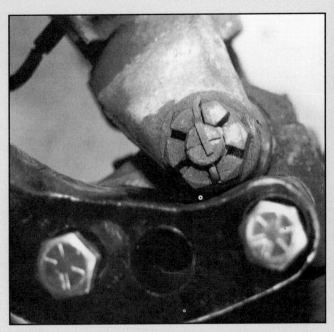

6. Use a pickle fork to remove the stock drag link, a hammer to remove the stock steering arm, and a grinder to make the raised Skyjacker steering arm clear the ball joint. You have to grind what seems like a lot off of the arm, but it isn't near the bolt holes and strength isn't affected.

7. Our tailpipe exited right where the new rear springs wanted to be, so out came the reciprocating saw. You may also run into problems with the front driveshaft hitting the crossover pipe, but our application had plenty of clearance.

8. The rear bolts spanked us good. After four hours of bashing with a 3-pound hammer, this was the only bolt we could free—right into the gas tank. Crap! We pushed it back in place and limped to M.I.T.

Do It Yourself?

We've got to say this up front. M.I.T. saved our bacon—period. It's no secret we're always in a last-minute thrash to get our junk running. In this case, we were heading to Moab in a matter of days and needed the springs installed so we could order driveshafts. With deadlines looming, we called Jeff Sugg at M.I.T., who cleared a lift for us and pulled master technician Rick Dziezyk off of what he was doing to cut and torch our old springs off. There was no other way those suckers were coming out. Dziezyk also pressed out our wasted rear shackle bushings and installed new ones. The bushings were completely fused to the shackles and almost stalled a 25-ton hydraulic press. We would never have been able to get the rear suspension off in our driveway without renting a torch. However, since we're amateurs with a torch—the spring hangers are right near the plastic gas tank and we don't like being on fire—taking our junk to the professionals seemed the prudent thing to do. While the Dodge was on the M.I.T. lift, they let us install our rear springs and take care of a few other odds and ends.

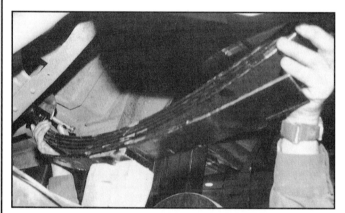

Skyjacker uses 4-inch lift springs in conjunction with the factory blocks for Ramchargers. Using the 6-inch spring causes the vehicle to sit ass-high.

Six States took our info over the phone and sent us front and rear driveshafts with CVs, 1310 yolks for the front Dana 44 and rear Dana 60, and a 1330 CV yolk for the NP208 transfer case. Six States also included all of the U-bolts and hardware.

Who's your daddy? The Stockton wheels look killer and the 4-inch backspacing keeps the 315/75/16 Geolandar MTs out of the steering and suspension components. The Yokohamas run smooth and quiet on the highway, have a nice bulge when aired down, and grip like Mama Cass in a candy factory. We're really happy with the wheel and tire combo.

27 Curing Axlewrap

By John Cappa
Photography by John Cappa

Around the office we joke about creating a No Traction idiot light. As crazy as it might sound, it could be helpful in traversing slippery terrain. The light would be connected to sensors on the suspension, in the differentials, and on the throttle. These sensors would determine the condition where the most traction is obtained before tire-spin occurs (threshhold traction).

In reality, most vehicles depend on the driver's senses and input to provide the optimum amount of power to the wheels for maximum traction. However, some suspension systems are superior to others for getting the power to the ground. That doesn't mean you should rip out the boingers in your leaf-sprung truck and install a complex jungle-gym of bars to maintain grip.

In fact, the most common rear suspension is a leaf-sprung solid-axle type. Unfortunately, this is the only kind of suspension that has axlewrap. Pickup trucks are especially prone to wrapup because there is little weight over the rear wheels. But there are many ways to make leaf springs perform more effectively. Here's a look at some of the ways along with some of the more exotic suspension systems that cure the axlewrap dance.

Axlewrap

Axlewrap is one of the more annoying reasons for loss of traction. Common on soft, leaf-sprung suspensions, it is defined as the condition where the rotational load from the axle is placed on the leaf springs. It flexes them into an "S" shape, storing spring energy until the tires slip. The spring then releases the energy, which causes a bounce and tire spin—essentially a loss of traction.

This sequence wouldn't be that hard to control if it were a slow process, but it most often occurs under moderate to extreme throttle, giving it machine gun–like speed and repetition. Staying on the throttle in this condition could break axleshafts, driveshafts, U-joints, and other driveline components. It is also harmful to suspension components.

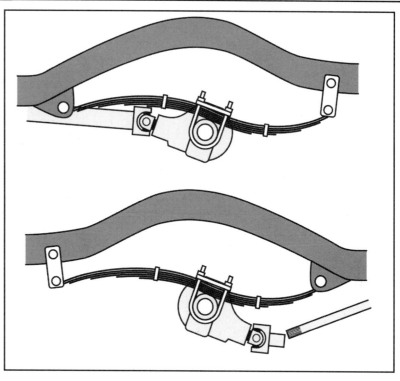

Several methods are used to control and eliminate the wrapping of the springs. If suspension flex is required for the type of 'wheeling encountered, special attention needs to be paid to the design of a traction system so that it doesn't limit or bind during axle articulation or travel cycling.

This Jeep incorporates some of the best methods for controlling axlewrap. The thick spring pack is difficult for the low-horsepower engine to wind into an "S" shape. Spring-under suspensions are less susceptible to axlewrap. The spring clips pictured are of the bolt type with the bolt removed for increased droop (downtravel). If wrapup were a problem, the bolts could be reinstalled or a clamp-type spring clip could be used.

Poorly designed or maladjusted traction links can cause binding or even breakage such as this broken rod-end on an aftermarket traction link. Bolt-on components like this are designed for specific lift kits and may not work properly in other applications.

The design of this fabricated traction bar harnesses the rotational force of the axlehousing and converts it to an up-and-down motion, as the arrows indicate. To maintain flexibility in the suspension, only one link is used. It is bushing-mounted at both ends and has a greaseable slip-joint to allow for articulation and suspension travel.

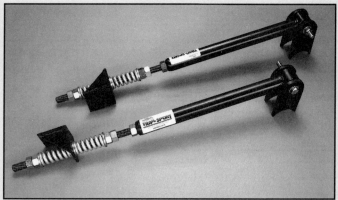

These Trail Traction bars from Trail Sport utilize two heavy springs in a floating design to minimize wrapup while maintaining a compliant suspension. The bars convert the rotational energy of the axle to forward-and-aft movement. This movement is controlled by the small coils that can be adjusted to the desired preload. The tighter the springs are set, the less wrapup the axle will have. However, if they are set too tight, suspension travel and articulation will suffer.

The Trail Sport bars can be installed on front or rear axles. As the throttle is applied, rotational force is placed on the housing. This force is converted to compression that collapses the small coils on the bars, controlling axlewrap. The arrows indicate the movement.

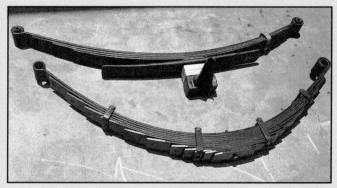

Using lift blocks in the rear increases the leverage that the axle has on the leaf springs, thus intensifying axlewrap. The stock Ford spring (top) combined with the factory block and an aftermarket lift block makes for an unsafe combination. A safer way to lift the rear of the truck is to use custom springs (bottom) that eliminate the need for blocks. This custom pack may look heavily arched and stiff, but each leaf is very thin, giving a smooth ride.

Double or military-spring eyes help control axlewrap. An added bonus is that if the main leaf should break, the wrapped leaf can hold the spring together until it can be replaced or repaired. Double wrap eyes will keep the spring from fanning out (spreading apart), so suspension flexibility will be reduced.

A snail wrap uses three leaves to create the eye of the spring. Two wrap from the bottom, and one wraps from the top. This design is used to control axlewrap on high-horsepower vehicles with soft, long-travel suspensions.

A four-link quarter-elliptic suspension uses four bars to locate the axle throughout its travel, preventing axle wrapup. This custom-built setup isn't cheap, but it offers lots of movement. Many new-truck manufacturers are using similar link systems on their 4x4s to achieve a smooth ride and increase wheel travel.

The suspension shown is a one-link design. It also has a Panhard rod to control side-to-side movement. The link pictured is a one-piece wishbone that is welded directly to the axle. This eliminates wrapup altogether.

The frame-mounted pivot is a ball-and-socket design. This allows the axle to articulate to extreme angles without binding. The ball is held in place by the six-bolt retainer that sandwiches the adjusting shims. When the ball or socket begins to show signs of wear (clunking), shims can be removed to tighten it up.

Several types of spring clips are available. Both of these are clamp-type, but the one on the left is loose-fitting. This allows the spring leaves to fan out (separate) increasing articulation. The clamp on the right is tightly wrapped. These can limit travel but will also help control axlewrap.

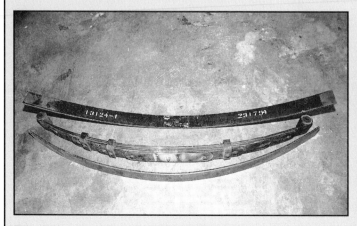

Thin, full-length add-a-leaves lift the vehicle while maintaining a good ride. They also help control axlewrap by increasing the spring rate. However, they don't control wrapup as well as thick, short add-a-leaves, which stiffen the ride.

The more arch a spring has, the less likely it is to succumb to wrapup. A heavy load compressing the springs can also make it more difficult for the axle to twist them.

Tires

The first thing most of us think of when it comes to traction is tires. We imagine a big fat knobby mud tire to be the ultimate in traction. But that's not always the case. If it were, drag racers would be using them instead of slicks. The type of terrain encountered is very important to consider when picking tires for maximum traction.

Not everyone agrees on the best tires for the same terrain. If you walked through the pit at a mud race, you'd be amazed by the rubber combinations.

Ross Early of Eaton, Colorado, has a '77 Chevy Blazer with a GM 12-bolt rear and a Dana 44 front. He runs 38.5x11 Swamper Boggers in front and 16x35x15s in the rear. The 35s sport 6-inch-wide wheels, while the 38s have 10-inchers, which he says keep the back tires running in the same rut as the front.

George Gallegos of Fountain, Colorado, has 38.5-inch Swamper TSLs all around his '73 Chevy Blazer and uses stock rims, but he has found that tall, skinny tires bite better with more air pressure, so he runs them at 15-25 psi, depending on the bog conditions.

Jim Bramford of Kearney, Nebraska, who drives a '90 Chevy S-10 Extended Cab, prefers a wide tire because he feels he can get on top of the mud. His suggestion is that if you have a light truck, go with wider tires. If the truck's heavy, go with narrow ones. Bramford thinks the Swampers are best for mud. When it's really wet he runs 3 psi at all four corners, and when it's harder he runs 5 psi.

Finally, Ted Farmer of Lakewood, Colorado, has two sets of tires for his '77 Ford F-250, both Ground Hawgs: 40-inchers on 12-inch-wide wheels and 9.75x16.5s on regular modular wheels. He thinks Hawgs are far better than Swampers for mud, since they have directional, open lugs and last a whole lot longer.

On just about any terrain, the wrong tire can cause slippage, which leads to increased axlewrap. Along with the best tire for your terrain, the correct air pressure also helps to prevent slippage by providing a larger footprint on the ground.

The Torque Arm

The Easy Way to Eliminate Axlewrap

By Cole Quinnell
Photography by Cole Quinnell and John Cappa

28

Spring-overs almost always result in axlewrap. It's a fact of life—especially if you use stock Jeep Wrangler springs. These springs give you an ultra-cush ride and unbelievable flex when mounted on top of the axle, but they just can't control the power input. Add a potent V-8 and you better buy stock in Dana Spicer to help offset your spending on U-joints. You'll also wear out the springs faster than you can believe, and you're likely to spit out a rear driveshaft or two.

The age-old fix has been to construct some sort of traction bar, but that usually takes quite a bit of trial and error, and results in suspension bind and limitation of rear-axle articulation. So what's a spring-over addict to do? Use one of Uncle Sam's shackle-mounted traction bars, that's what.

Sam Patton of Sam's Off-Road knows plenty about spring-overs and axlewrap. He's been performing spring-over conversions for more than 15 years and the type of 'wheeling he's accustomed to requires plenty of horsepower. A few years ago he developed a traction device for his own rig and thought that other throttle-happy owners of spring-overed rigs could benefit from the product. It was designed for a CJ-7, but will fit just about any vehicle.

We've seen Sam's CJ-7 work on the trail. We've also owned a few spring-overs and had plenty of tries at developing a traction bar. So we were anxious to try Sam's, which promised to be an easy install with all the engineering already figured out.

The device looks a lot like a ladder bar used on drag race cars. It is meant

Here's the deal: for $295, Sam's Off-Road will send you a traction bar made from 1-inch, 0.120-inch wall DOM tubing, a shackle, and a Rock Slider shackle mount. The traction bar has three greaseable Johnny Joints built into it for maximum twist potential. The shackle accommodates forward and rearward axle movement, while controlling axlehousing rotation.

The axle mount is cut to fit the 3-inch-diameter axle tubing used on Dana 44s. Our Jeep has a Dana 60 so we used an angle grinder to open up the half-circles slightly to fit the tubes. You'll at least want to sand the paint off this mount for a clean weld.

to be welded onto the rear axletube and the other end is attached to a crossmember via a shackle. But its function is not as simple as it seems. The traction bar controls axlewrap by preventing the axletube from rotating under power. This keeps the springs from bending into an "S" and snapping back into place. You can accomplish the same thing with two solid links (one above, and the other below the axletube) mounted solidly at both ends, but that wouldn't allow the axle to move forward or backward, which occurs when the spring compresses and droops,

moving the spring shackles. The Sam's Off-Road traction bar handles this with the use of a shackle at the front mount. No matter how hard the axle tries to rotate the bar up, the shackle stops it and converts the force to downward pressure on the tires for more traction. To deal with articulation without limiting it, Patton uses Johnny Joints at the axle and the traction-bar shackle. These allow 30 degrees of movement before binding. Depending on how close you mount it to the center of the axle, this practically guarantees free movement as the axle articulates.

We are the worst skeptics in the industry, so we insisted on installing one on a spring-over Jeep. While the installation does require welding and you have to construct a mount for the traction-bar shackle, installation was quite easy. Our Jeep has a 380hp engine, stock Wrangler springs, a Dana 60 axle, 5.13 gears, and a stickshift. That's about the worst combination you could ask for when trying to avoid axlewrap.

The Sam's Off-Road traction bar did everything it was supposed to and nothing it wasn't. On loose hillclimbs and in sandy washes, the pinion stayed where we set it, and axlewrap was nonexistent, no matter how hard we stood on the throttle. Furthermore, the Jeep scored over 1,000 on a 30-degree RTI ramp and, more importantly, worked awesome off-road. Now that's the right way to get rid of axlewrap.

Mock up your front mount and the axle mount with the vehicle sitting at static ride height. If you had your spring perches welded on with more than 1 degree of downward pinion angle, you may wish to install shims, bringing it to zero before installing the traction bar. The shackle is mounted so that the traction bar will be above the shackle mount.

Position the traction bar as close to the center of the axle as possible, but the center section and obstacles at the front of the bar will probably force the bar to one side or the other. Tack-weld the bar in place, double-check your mounts, then fully weld the traction-bar mount to the axlehousing.

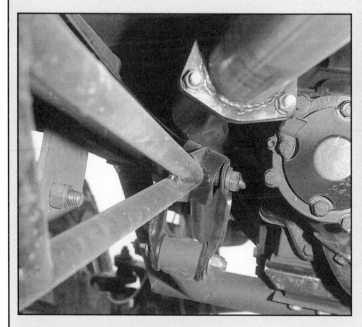

We built a tubular front mount off the transfer-case crossmember. Instead of using the Rock Slider mount provided, we used 1 3/4-inch tubing and polyurethane Wrangler leaf-spring bushings for our front mount. You'll want the shackle to be perpendicular to the arm when the vehicle is sitting on level ground.

The beauty of this traction system is that there's nothing for you to figure out. Install it as we've shown and your axlewrap problems are over. We've beat the snot out of the Jeep in sand and over rocks, and driven it on the street without any noticeable drawbacks. And we don't miss the axlewrap at all.

29

Pony Power Steering

A New Option for Early Broncos

By Craig Perronne
Photography by Craig Perronne

If you drive a manual-steering Bronco then wrestling with your steering wheel is a common occurrence. Getting around town involves lots of effort and tackling a tight trail is completely out of the question. Having power steering is a dream that every manual-boxed Pony owner has nightly.

Two options used to be available for early Broncos ('66–'77) to convert to power steering. The first involved grafting a F-150 two-wheel-drive box into position. These boxes use a long sector shaft that occasionally snaps when subjected to heavy off-road use. The length of the sector shaft also causes the box to hang down 7 1/4 inches below the frame, which means that a suspension lift is necessary to

have decent steering geometry. Another drawback to the F-150 box is that it mounts to the inside of the frame instead of the stock outside of the frame location, which means a custom drag link needs to be fabricated.

The other option is to find an early Bronco equipped with power steering and cannibalize it. However, this is close to impossible nowadays as these boxes are becoming harder to locate. The stock boxes are adequate for most use but have been known to crack the cases. They are also hampered by the original Ford power-steering pump, which does not supply that much pressure.

New on the scene is the James Duff power-steering conversion that

combines the best of both worlds. It uses a Saginaw power-steering box built by AGR that bolts to the outside of the frame and only hangs down 2 1/2 inches, eliminating the need for a custom drag link or suspension lift. The Saginaw box is only 3 1/3 turns lock-to-lock compared to the four turns of the F-150 box and six or four turns ('76–'77 Broncos) of the stock Bronco. A Saginaw pump, also built by AGR, is used to provide plenty of pressure to the box. Both AGR pieces are only available through James Duff and cannot be purchased through AGR. Best of all, the James Duff kit simply bolts into place and can be installed by the average mechanic.

Here is the James Duff power-steering kit ready to go on. It is a complete kit that comes ready to install and transform your manual-steering steed into an easy-to-maneuver pony. On the right and underneath the plastic is the heart of the kit: the AGR box and pump. The rest is the brackets, pulleys, hoses, and additional hardware necessary to convert to power steering.

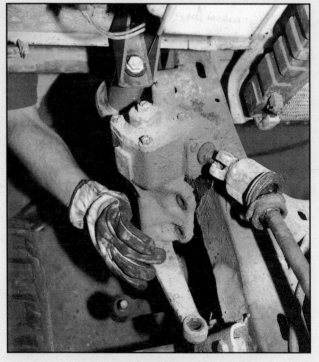

First to come off was the original manual-steering box. The three bolts that attach it to the frame are removed and then it comes right off. The Bronco's owner was more than happy to see it go.

The next step was to put the power-steering box into position. Measurements can then be taken to drill the extra hole that needs to be put into the frame.

After the measurements are taken, the frame can then be drilled for the new hole required for the Saginaw box. Also included in the kit is a crush sleeve that is installed at this time to add extra strength to the frame. Once the hole is drilled, the box can be put back into position and bolted to the frame.

We also opted to install the power-steering box truss. That is a good idea for anyone who plans to use the Bronco off road, especially with large tires and a front locker. The truss uses one more bolt (the upper-right one without a bolt in it) to help spread load out across the frame. It can also be used with the stock Bronco power steering.

Next to come out was the radiator. After it's removed, the fan, the water pump pulley, and the crankshaft pulley can all be yanked.

The original crankshaft pulley and water pump pulley need to be replaced with double-sheaved units to spin the new power-steering pump. You can either dig around in a junkyard to find some or get them through James Duff. The Duff units are underdrive pulleys so the belt supplied with the kit will not work. A quick trip to the local auto parts store solved this problem.

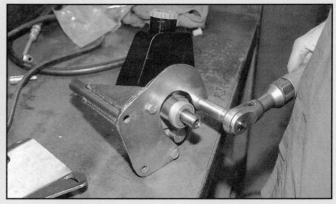

A special AGR pump is used along with the AGR box. It supplies more pressure (1,500 psi) than the standard power-steering pump to provide easier steering. A horseshoe-shaped adapter is attached to the front of the box, and this cadmium-plated bracket then attaches to it.

A threaded piece of rod is then screwed into the bottom of the head to mount the pump. We initially screwed it into the hole on the inboard side of the head (pictured) but then quickly realized it was the wrong hole. The location of the right hole to use is on the outboard side roughly where the fuel filter is on this Bronco.

The two cadmium-plated brackets supplied with the kit are then used to mount the pump to the engine. One bracket attaches to the pump (previously pictured) and then slides over the piece of threaded rod while the other attaches to the water-pump bolts.

After everything was test-fitted, the power-steering pump pulley was taken back out and the pulley was installed onto it. Use a pulley installer, not a hammer, to put the pulley into position. The two lines going from the pump to the box were also installed at this time.

The Off-Road Unlimited crew realized early on that the stock one-piece steering shaft would probably not hook back up to the new box. Our test Bronco was equipped with a 2-inch body lift and the shaft, low and behold, was off by about 2 inches. For vehicles without a body lift or for later Broncos with a two-piece steering shaft this is not a problem.

A couple of options exist to solve the steering-shaft dilemma, such as notching the firewall, or using the Flaming River joint offered by James Duff, but the ORU crew decided the best route was to build a new shaft. The original steering shaft was cut out of the way with a Sawzall, leaving a little bit of the original shaft to work with.

A quick call to Lee Manufacturing and a couple of steering joints were on their way. The bottom joint is splined on one end to attach to the splines of the box and smooth on the other to attach to the shaft while the top joint is smooth on both sides. For vehicles that do not need a different shaft, Duff offers a bell coupler to attach the stock shaft to the box.

133

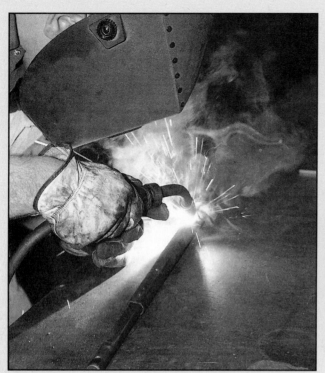

The use of steering joints also required using a shaft with a slip joint. One was quickly located and cannibalized out of a Chevy that was lying around. The steering joints were then welded and bolted to the new shaft. Figuring out the shaft and fabricating took the majority of the time for the install. It was also the only part that involved a welder.

Since our test Bronco was going to be used hard, a cooler was installed to keep the power-steering fluid happy. This cooler from Flex-a-lite was put into position on the driver side of the front core. It is actually a transmission cooler and is probably overkill, but we liked it because it came with a fan that can be used to help draw air at slow speeds.

Stay in Control
Currie's Jeep Steering Upgrade

By David Kennedy
Photography by David Kennedy

Quick, take your hands off the steering wheel and try to drive even 10 feet down your favorite trail using just the throttle (clutch) and brakes. No, you can't use your knees to turn the steering wheel either! Bet you can't do it. Shoot, you'd be lucky to make it down your driveway if you couldn't use the steering wheel to aim your rig.

Now imagine you weren't just engaging in an exercise. Think how it would be if something in your steering linkage broke and you lost all

directional control of your rig. If it happened on the trail it would be downright scary. If it happened on the ride home at 65 mph…well, we won't even think those kind of thoughts.

Here at *4-Wheel & Off-Road* we're always looking for new products that will add function, safety, and off-road worthiness to your 4x4. (Please, no thanks necessary—just doing our jobs.) So when we were hanging out at Currie Enterprises in Anaheim, California—drooling over some incredible axle assemblies—we

noticed some beefy steering linkages under Currie's competition vehicles, and we thought it would be the perfect thing for the Jeep junkies out there. Currie assured us they had broken just about everything that could be broken on a Jeep, and that this new steering kit would make a great addition to any XJ, ZJ, or TJ out on the trail. We would have to agree, so we shot a few photos and asked a few questions as they installed the new steering setup on their in-house go-fast truck.

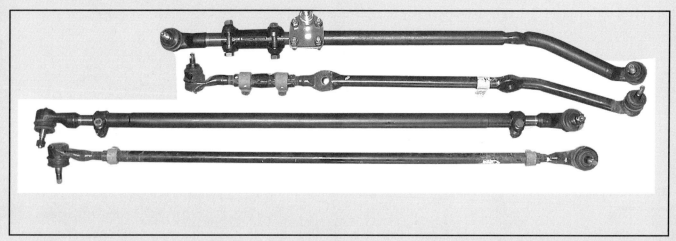

The Currie heavy duty Jeep steering upgrade is made of 1 1/4-inch chrome moly steel. It fits '97–'01 Wranglers, '84–'01 Cherokees and '93–'98 Grand Cherokees.

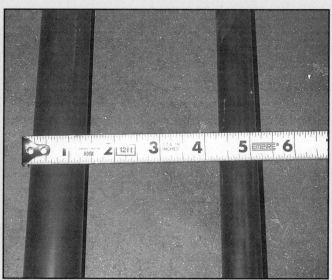

The Curries know how to break Jeeps. They torture their Fire Ant TJ in ARCA rockcrawling competitions and pound on a yellow Cherokee in JeepSpeed desert racing. They know what parts break and how to build new stuff to make it stronger. Their new steering kit was created because they kept snapping the stock drag link where the threaded rod enters the adjuster (arrow).

The Currie steering shafts are stronger because they use 1 1/4-inch chrome-moly tubing and beefier tie-rod ends to replace the 7/8-inch-diameter stock pieces. The stock rods hold up fine with 31s, but add a front locker and some 35s, and a driver can wreck stock steering faster than you can say, "Hello, parts department?"

The beauty of this kit is the fact that it works on Cherokees, TJs, and ZJ Grand Cherokees. The tie rod and drag link bolt on just like the stock parts do, so it's a super-easy upgrade. The kit comes with all new tie-rod ends, adjusters, and rods to replace your original equipment that was probably all loose anyway. Here you can see the kit being installed on their Cherokee built for desert racing.

The factory drag link is bowed to clear the lower spring bucket and sway bar mount. The new Currie arm is also bent to give additional clearance in this area because they found the stock rod would hit the axle when the suspension is crossed up.

Currie eliminates the hole in the drag link that the factory steering stabilizer mounts to. Instead the Currie kit uses a clamp-on style mount that lets you retain this feature without weakening the stock shaft.

31 AGR's Rock Ram Steering System

By Christian Hazel
Photography by John Cappa

We've run across plenty of serious trail rigs running homemade hydraulic ram assists. They make it possible to turn really big tires off road and take most of the stress off the steering box mount. But once you find a ram cylinder that will work with the pressure your power steering pump puts out, make brackets, cobble together the lines, and ensure that the steering box won't get toasted, you've invested some pretty serious time and effort.

After ripping the steering box off the frame of our Project 14-Day Flattie, we knew we wanted a hydraulic ram to take the pressure off of our mount and

to make steering a one-handed affair, even in the most evil of rocks. Rather than go through the uncertain steps outlined above, we simply dove into AGR's catalog for some one-stop shopping. AGR offers its Rock Ram System, which includes everything you need except the steering pump reservoir and a welder. For about $1,200, the kit comes with one of AGR's quick 16:1 ratio Rock Ram steering boxes, a Super Pump, a Rock Ram hydraulic assist cylinder, universal mounts, a hose kit, and a reservoir extension and cap.

Off road, the results were just what we expected. The steering wheel could

be turned with one finger, even with the front ARB engaged and the tires at 8 psi in a field of boulders. On road we experienced a slight lag between steering input and ram actuation. We haven't figured it out yet, but we're betting it has something to do with the length of our pitman arm. A longer arm will increase the quickness of the steering, but the ram doesn't know that, so it's fighting to catch up. We'll work it out and bring you the info in the future. One thing is for sure: We're totally spoiled now and are wishing that we could one-finger-steer all of our rigs.

For You If...

• You run tires way bigger than 35s
• You drive in the rocks
• You do a lot of tight, technical driving
• Your stock steering system is shot and you're stepping up to high-zoot components anyway
• You have a fullsize or sprung-under rig with lots of room to mount the ram

Not for You If...

• You only run 35-inch tires or smaller
• You don't run a front locker
• You don't do much hard-core wheeling
• You can't afford the approximate $1,200 price tag
• You have a rig with a narrow axle or frame, or engine components make mounting the ram difficult

Normally, the AGR high-zoot steering box mounts directly in place of the old Saginaw box, but we needed to build a new mount because ours tore off the frame. The box is lightly valved with a 16:1 ratio.

You must transfer the pulley and reservoir from the old power steering pump to the new AGR unit. The new pump supplies enough pressure to keep the box and ram happy. The stock unit wouldn't even come close.

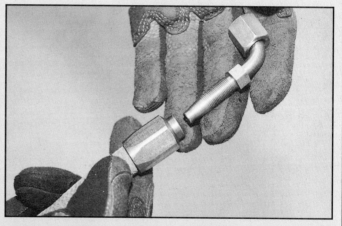

Assemble the fittings to the hoses and connect the pump, box, and ram according to the instructions. You'll want to take the hoses into consideration when locating the position of the ram.

When locating the ram, choose a position that allows it to travel through the entire steering range without bottoming. You don't want the ram acting as your steering stop. With the mounts tacked on, we bolted on the ram and cycled the steering one last time to ensure the steering wasn't limited before burning in the final welds.

After finish-welding the mounts, we hit them with some paint and reinstalled the ram. Fill the system with fluid and bleed it by turning the wheel lock-to-lock with the engine running. Check the fluid level frequently while doing this to avoid burning out the pump.

What's better, bolt-on or built-up? Most people who are using leaf springs on their Jeeps, Land Cruisers, and Scouts have at least thought about a spring-over, and many have actually done the conversion. Is it really cheaper and better than a lift kit? We wanted to find out.

For this comparo we built two almost identical '77 CJ-7s. They both have factory T-18 trannies and Dana 20 transfer cases. The axles are mostly stock AMC 20 and Dana 30 units. They even have the same 33-inch Goodyear MT/R tires on Center Line 15x8 Polaris wheels. The front and rear differentials are locked with Powertrax No-Slips and have 4.10 gears from Drivetrain Direct,

and both Jeeps are ugly. The only difference lies in the engines. The spring-over Jeep (we'll call this one Stalky) has a carbureted 304 V-8, and the other (Stumpy) has a fuel injected 258. Hold yer britches, this test isn't about horsepower or idle quality. It's about the good, the bad, and the ugly truth of 'over and 'under suspensions.

We ordered almost all of the optional parts for our Superlift kit. Regular price for all these parts is around $600. Normal labor cost for installation would be about $300. Since only regular handtools are needed for the install we opted to do it ourselves.

Stalky (left) turned out to be about 1 1/4 inches taller than Stumpy. After only one day of off-road testing Stalky's suspension had sagged 1/4 inch. Flexing stock springs means great suspension travel, but quickly wears out the springs. We suspect it will sag even farther in the future. Our bolt-on lift kit maintained its height after the initial break-in.

In the Ring

Stumpy received a complete 4-inch Superlift suspension system. The springs, spring bushings, and U-bolts came in the kit. We also ordered most of the optional parts, which included longer braided stainless brake lines, shackle bushings, a pitman arm, and shocks. Rocky Mountain Suspension Products provided all the Superlift products and recommended the optional equipment to maximize the bolt-on lift. The kit cost around $400, and all of the optional parts added another $200. Labor to install a kit such as this is about $300 at most 4x4 shops. We opted to do it ourselves, thank you very much. The parts bolted on with common handtools, two jackstands, and a floor jack.

Stalky already had a spring-over when we bought it. It did need some tuning but most of the work was completed. To perform a spring-over you will need four new perches, a welder (as in machine), a competent welder (as in person), and stock springs, in addition to common handtools. Seem cheap, simple, and easy enough? Not quite. You will also need extended brake lines, longer shocks, custom shock mounts, a pitman arm, and possible driveshaft modifications. A traction bar will undoubtedly be added to this list and the drag link may need to be modified to keep it from hitting the passenger-side spring. Other vehicles may require more or less. Still think that a spring-over is cheaper than a lift kit? Think again. The spring perches are cheap at about $15 a pair, but all the additional parts make a spring-over expensive. We were quoted between $750 and $1,400 for a drive-in drive-out spring-over lift. It would be even more expensive to have a traction bar of some sort built.

To get the full flex from Stalky we added longer front shock towers from 4 Wheeler's Supply, and Rancho 9000 shocks all the way around. To keep things equal we performed the same mods on Stumpy. The front shocks on Stumpy had to be a little shorter than Stalky's or they would have bottomed out at full bump. The rear shocks are identical in length but Stalky has new mounts welded to the axle.

We originally tried to use the factory shackles (junk). Stumpy broke one early on so we replaced the shackles on both Jeeps with heavy-duty Daystar 1-inch lift pieces with greaseable bolts as a preventive measure. These were also ordered through Rocky Mountain Suspension Products.

Stalky had 13 1/2 inches of clearance under the front axletubes. With the springs and spring plates up and out of the way, rocks could more easily pass below.

Stumpy only had 10 1/2 inches below the front spring plate. However, the tie rod is less vulnerable in this area because it is protected by the leaf spring. The leaves also act as skidplates to help the axle up and over rocks.

A drop Superlift pitman arm was installed on Stalky to correct the steering angles. At full droop the drag link hit the passenger-side leaf spring. This can be remedied with a custom bent drag link.

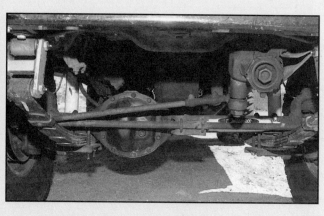

We originally installed a drop pitman arm on Stumpy, but it seemed to cause more bumpsteer than it cured. The clearance at the differentials on both vehicles is the same since both vehicles have the same tires, wheels, and axles.

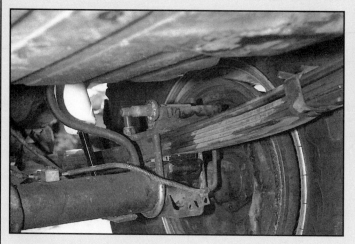

Under the rear of Stalky (left) there were 13 1/2 inches of clearance. A custom shock mount had to be welded to the housing because of the spring-over. The original mount can be spotted on the now flipped-over spring plate. Notice that the hard brake line is in a vulnerable position below the spring. With 9 inches of clearance under the rear spring plates, Stalky (right) sure loses this contest. The shock is also mounted precariously low, although the brake line is in a safe place.

Because the lift springs increase in length as they are compressed, the rear axle will move to the rear on Stumpy (left). The tire rubs on the back of the fender at full stuff. Stalky (right) has the opposite problem. The springs flex into negative arch when compressed, which effectively shortens the length of the springs. The tire hits the front part of the fender and body mount. Pick your poison.

The tires rubbed on the front shocks and mounts on both Jeeps. Wider axles are probably the only real solution to this problem. This is perhaps the reason these mounts weren't offered until 1982 when the Wide-track axles found their way under CJs.

To eliminate driveline vibrations, ol' Stalky needed a CV driveshaft. This unit alone cost almost as much as our bolt-on lift kit. The rear driveshafts in both Jeeps are 27 inches long. Stalky's front shaft is 32 inches and Stumpy's is 31. In either case, the stock front driveshaft will work.

On the trail, Stumpy often lifted a tire but it never slowed down thanks to Powertrax No-Slip lockers front and rear.

Stalky was able to keep the tires planted thanks to a more compliant suspension. However, with lockers in the front and back of both vehicles this didn't appear to be an advantage.

With 14 psi in all four tires we headed up the middle of a 23-degree ramp with Stumpy. It scored a 628. Normal wheelbase for a CJ-7 is 93 1/2 inches. With the Superlift 4-inch springs, it became 94 inches.

With the same tire pressure and tire positioning on the ramp, Stalky ramped a 709. The wheelbase is 94 1/2 inches, a whole inch longer than stock. This could be attributed to sagging springs.

We drove both vehicles through a nasty rock gully and neither seemed to have an advantage. Stalky did have 1 1/4 inches more clearance at the rocker panel. This wasn't enough to make an earth-shattering difference in trail performance, but it does help.

Stalky's suspension was more susceptible to leaning around corners and swaying over bumps. These characteristics tipped the Jeep onto its side around this sidehilled corner, which wasn't nearly as exciting in Stumpy.

Hard braking was tolerable in both vehicles. Stalky's frontend dove where Stumpy's stayed level due to a firmer suspension. However, the ride in Stalky was considerably smoother than in Stumpy.

Stumpy (shown) could sit and spin the tires all day without a trace of bouncing. Stalky had noticeable wheelhop in the sand. It wasn't bad enough that the driveshaft would bind, but a traction bar would have been a good idea.

By the end of the day the stock springs on Stalky were beginning to sag and had bent into negative arch. This can lead to a significant loss of lift or possibly spring breakage within a short amount of time.

And the Winner Is...

The winner and loser of this test are not as black and white as most people would want to believe. More than cost and flexibility needs to be considered to pick a winner. With lockers in both axles, lifting a tire is hardly a concern. The spring-over is probably the better choice for the individual who can do the work himself and plans on tinkering and constantly changing things. The performance of the suspension will depend on the competence of the installer. The dilemma lies in the fact that a spring-over rides smoother than most lift kits. Contrary to popular belief, a spring-over will cost you more money in the long run.

A bolt-on kit, such as our Superlift kit, can be installed by just about anyone. Once it's on you can pretty much forget about it. In the scheme of things, a bolt-on kit is the more cost effective option. It may ride a little firmer, but that's a small price to pay for worry-free wheeling.

33 Suspension Tips for Flex

By John Cappa
Photography by *4-Wheel & Off-Road* **Staff**

Functional suspensions have come into their own. Long gone are rock-hard lift springs with limited movement. Traveling to all kinds of different events and shops can sometimes make us a little jaded at times. We often forget about Suspension 101 and head straight for the advanced custom stuff. There has also been a flood of bolt-on trinkets that add flex, some of which frighten even us for street use. What we've put together here is several modifications that will improve suspension performance. Whether your suspension is completely bolt-on or totally fabricated, there should be something to give you that extra edge.

Lift springs have arc to them; they will get longer as they compress. Short factory shackles will often bottom-out on the frame in this situation. For the best performance from your lift springs, use shackles that are about 1 inch longer than stock. They will also provide about 1/2 inch of lift.

Everyone knows that rubber bushings are more flexible than urethane, but we doubt the extra flex outweighs the benefits of practically bombproof urethane. These urethane units seem to flex just fine. However, one of them is cracked. Greasable shackles and spring pivots may be messy but they improve the ride and flexibility.

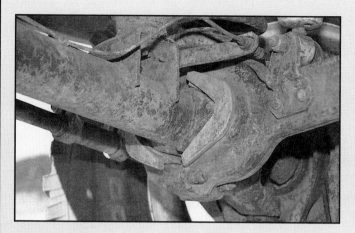

Ford C-bushings are one place where we're not sure urethane is better. Urethane's firm characteristics can limit articulation because of the suspension design. When articulated, the axlehousing effectively becomes a giant torsion bar, except it doesn't give. Rubber bushings allow slightly more movement.

Rather than replace Ford C-bushings with degreed urethane units—to compensate for a lift—you can lengthen the radius arms. Lengthening the arms will also alleviate some of the bind that limits articulation.

Undoing modifications can increase flex too. This ladder bar setup would work great at the drag strip to eliminate wheelhop. However, in the dirt and rocks your suspension will have a bad case of rigor mortis. Traction bars should be inspected to make sure they don't bind.

If you're into speed and jumps, these coil inserts are for you. They go inside the coils and offer cushy progressive bumpstops, making airtime landings less jarring. They aren't the hot setup for crawling since they will limit slow-speed compression.

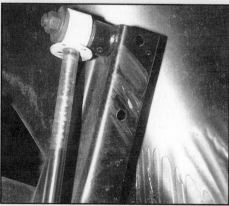

Frame additions that lower the spring and shackle mounts are an easy way to obtain a little lift without caster or pinion angle change. We aren't big fans of this mod, but it is acceptable when used in conjunction with custom-built leaf-spring suspensions that have well-thought-out steering and driveshaft angles.

Often what limits an otherwise flexible suspension is the shocks. You could have all sorts of spring-over or link-suspension widgetry and it won't do you any good if the shocks bottom or top out. Longer shocks and custom mounts may be needed.

If you are building custom links for your suspension, you may want to consider rod ends. They can function with more misalignment than rubber or urethane bushings. The degree of misalignment that a rod end can tolerate depends on its design and the mount that is used.

Incorrect bumpstop placement can cause hard bottoming or even limit travel. Check to see that bumpstops hit when they should. Full bump when articulated is different than full bump of the whole axle. Check both.

Mounting the shocks in this fashion (angled toward the axle center) will not counter sway. However, more travel can be obtained with a shorter shock. If a shock is mounted at 45 degrees it will only compress about 1/2 inch for every 1 inch of suspension travel. You could effectively turn your 8-inch stroke shock into a 16-inch travel magnate.

A better way to mount the shocks is in line with the frame, but at an angle (forward or back). Most truck manufacturers employ this design. The valving of the shocks needs to be firmer if they are angled rather than mounted perpendicular to the frame and axle. Adjustable shocks have an advantage over others when building custom mounts such as this.

Source Index

AGR Inc.
800/662-3649
www.agrsteering.com

Autofab
10996 N. Woodside Ave.
Santee, CA 92071
619/562-1740
www.autofab.com

ARB Accessories/
Old Man Emu Springs
20 S. Spokane St.
Seattle, WA 98134
888/427-2872
206/264-1669

Baja Racing Products
1040 S. Main St.
Fallbrook, CA 92028
760/723-2117
www.bajaconcepts.com

Bilstein
8845 Rehco Rd.
San Diego, CA 92121
800/537-1085
www.bilstein.com

Center Line Performance Wheels
13521 Freeway Dr.
Santa Fe Springs, CA 90670
310/921-9637

Currie Enterprises
714/528-6957
www.currieenterprises.com

Daystar Products
841 S. 71st Ave.
Phoenix, AZ 85043
800/595-7659
www.daystarproducts.com

Deaver Spring
Mfg. Co.
902 E. Second St.
Santa Ana, CA 92701
714/542-3703

Drivetrain Direct
29792 Avenida De Las Banderas
Rancho Santa Margarita, CA 92688
888/584-4327
www.drivetraindirect.com

Edelbrock
310/781-2222
www.edelbrock.com

Eaton Detroit Spring
1555 Michigan Ave.
Detroit, MI 48216
313/963-3839

Explorer ProComp
2360 Boswell Rd.
Chula Vista, CA 91914
619/216-1444
www.explorerprocomp.com

Fabtech
877/4-FABTECH
www.fabtechmotorsports.com

Flex-a-lite
7213 45th St., Crt. E
Fife, WA 98424
253/922-2700

4 Wheeler's Supply
3530 E. Washington St.
Phoenix, AZ 85034
602/273-7195

4 Wheel Parts Performance Centers
801 W. Artesia Blvd.
Compton, CA 90220

800/421-1050
www.4wheelparts.com

4 Wheel Parts Wholesalers
801 W. Artesia Blvd.
Compton, CA 90220
800/421-1050
www.4wheelparts.com

Goodyear Tire & Rubber Co.
1144 E. Market St., Ste. 702
Akron, OH 44316
330/796-2121
www.goodyear.com

Intercomp Co.
14465 23rd Ave. N.
Minneapolis, MN 55447
612/476-2531

James Duff Enterprises
261340 Hwy. 101
Sequim, WA 98382
360/683-2160
www.jamesduff.com

JET Performance Products
17491 Apex Cir.
Huntington Beach,
CA 92647
714/848-5415
www.jetchip.com

King Off-Road
Racing Shocks
10402 Trask Ave., Unit C
Garden Grove, CA 92843
714/530-8701
www.kingshocks.com

Krupp Bilstein
of America
800/537-1085
www.bilstein.com

Lee Manufacturing Co.
11661 Pendleton St.
Sun Valley, CA 91352
818/768-0371

Mag-Hytec
818/786-8325
www.mag-hytec.com

Mickey Thompson Performance Tires
4670 Allen Rd.
Stow, OH 44224
330/928-9092

M.I.T.
1112 Pioneer Way
El Cajon, CA
619/579-7727

National Spring
1402 N. Magnolia Ave.
El Cajon, CA 92020
619/441-1901

National Tire
& Wheel
800/847-3287
www.ntwonline.com

Off Road Unlimited
40 E. Palm Ave.
Burbank, CA 91502
818/563-1208
www.offroadunlimited.com

Powertrax
245 Fischer Ave., Bldg. B4
Costa Mesa, CA 92626
800/578-1020
www.powertrax.com

Pro Comp Tire Co.
2758 Via Orange Way
Spring Valley, CA 91978
800/776-0767

Race Car Dynamics
619/588-4723
www.racecardynamics.com

Rancho Suspensions
500 N. Field Dr.
Lake Forest, IL 60045
847/482-5000
800/574-6257 (tech)

Rancho Suspension
6925 Atlantic Ave.
Long Beach, CA 90805
562/630-0700
www.gorancho.com

Rocky Mountain Suspension Products
P.O. Box 10098
2178 Hwy. 160B
Bayfield, CO 81122
800/521-4908
www.rockymountainsusp.com

Rough Country
1445 Hwy. 51 Bypass E.
Dyersburg, TN 38024
800/222-7023

Sam's Off-Road
4345 Southwest Blvd.
Tulsa, OK 74107
918/446-5535
www.samsoffroad.com

Skyjacker
P.O. 1678
212 Stevenson St.
West Monroe, LA 71294
318/388-0816
www.skyjacker.com

Stockton Wheel
648 W. Fremont St.
Stockton, CA 95203
209/464-7771

Superlift
211 Horn Ln.
West Monroe, LA 71292
800/551-4955
www.superlift.com

Sway-A-Way
20755 Marilla St.
Chatsworth, CA 91311
818/700-9712
www.swayaway.com

Tri-County Gear
1143 W. Second St.
Pomona, CA 91766
909/623-3373

T & J's 4-Wheel Drive Auto Center
1002 W. Collins
Orange, CA 92867
714/633-0991

Trail Master
420 Jay St.
Coldwater, MI 49036
517/278-4011

Tuff Country
4165 W. Nike Dr.
West Jordan City, UT 84088
800/288-2190
801/280-2777

Warn/Black Diamond
12900 SE Capps Rd.
Clackamas, OR 97015-8903
800/543-9276
888/722-6730

Weld Racing Wheel
800/676-9353 www.weldracing.com

Yokohama Tire Corporation
601 S. Acacia Ave.
Fullerton, CA 92813
800/423-4544

HANDBOOKS

Auto Electrical Handbook: 0-89586-238-7 or HP1238
Auto Upholstery & Interiors: 1-55788-265-7 or HP1265
Car Builder's Handbook: 1-55788-278-9 or HP1278
4-Wheel & Off-Road's Chassis & Suspension Handbook: 1-55788-406-4
The Lowrider's Handbook: 1-55788-383-1 or HP1383
Powerglide Transmission Handbook:1-55788-355-6 or HP1355
Turbo Hydramatic 350 Handbook: 0-89586-051-1 or HP1051
Welder's Handbook: 1-55788-264-9 or HP1264

BODYWORK & PAINTING

Automotive Detailing: 1-55788-288-6 or HP1288
Automotive Paint Handbook: 1-55788-291-6 or HP1291
Fiberglass & Composite Materials: 1-55788-239-8 or HP1239
Metal Fabricator's Handbook: 0-89586-870-9 or HP1870
Paint & Body Handbook: 1-55788-082-4 or HP1082
Pro Paint & Body: 1-55788-394-7
Sheet Metal Handbook: 0-89586-757-5 or HP1757

INDUCTION

Bosch Fuel Injection Systems: 1-55788-365-3 or HP1365
Holley 4150: 0-89586-047-3 or HP1047
Holley Carbs, Manifolds & F.I.: 1-55788-052-2 or HP1052
Rochester Carburetors: 0-89586-301-4 or HP1301
Turbochargers: 0-89586-135-6 or HP1135
Weber Carburetors: 0-89586-377-4 or HP1377

PERFORMANCE

Baja Bugs & Buggies: 0-89586-186-0 or HP1186
Big-Block Chevy Performance: 1-55788-216-9 or HP1216
Big-Block Mopar Performance: 1-55788-302-5 or HP1302
Bracket Racing: 1-55788-266-5 or HP1266
Brake Systems: 1-55788-281-9 or HP1281
Camaro Performance: 1-55788-057-3 or HP1057
Chassis Engineering: 1-55788-055-7 or HP1055
Chevy Trucks: 1-55788-340-8 or HP1340
Ford Windsor Small-Block Performance: 1-55788-323-8 or HP1323
4Wheel&Off-Road's Chassis & Suspension: 1-55788-406-4/HP1406
Honda/Acura Engine Performance: 1-55788-384-X or HP1384
High Performance Hardware: 1-55788-304-1 or HP1304
How to Hot Rod Big-Block Chevys: 0-912656-04-2 or HP104
How to Hot Rod Small-Block Chevys: 0-912656-06-9 or HP106
How to Hot Rod Small-Block Mopar Engines: 0-89586-479-7 or HP1479
How to Hot Rod VW Engines: 0-912656-03-4 or HP103
How to Make Your Car Handle: 0-912656-46-8 or HP146
John Lingenfelter: Modify Small-Block Chevy: 1-55788-238-X or HP1238
Mustang 5.0 Projects: 1-55788-275-4 or HP1275

Mustang Performance (Engines): 1-55788-193-6 or HP1193
Mustang Performance 2 (Chassis): 1-55788-202-9 or HP1202
Mustang Perf. Chassis, Suspension, Driveline Tuning: 1-55788-387-4
Mustang Performance Engine Tuning: 1-55788-387-4 or HP1387
1001 High Performance Tech Tips: 1-55788-199-5 or HP1199
Performance Ignition Systems: 1-55788-306-8 or HP1306
Small-Block Chevy Performance: 1-55788-253-3 or HP1253
Small Block Chevy Engine Buildups: 1-55788-400-5 or HP1400
LS1/LS6 Small-Block Chevy Performance: 1-55788-407-2 or HP1407

ENGINE REBUILDING

Engine Builder's Handbook: 1-55788-245-2 or HP1245
How to Rebuild Small-Block Chevy LT-1/LT-4: 1-55788-393-9/HP1393
Rebuild Air-Cooled VW Engines: 0-89586-225-5 or HP1225
Rebuild Big-Block Chevy Engines: 0-89586-175-5 or HP1175
Rebuild Big-Block Ford Engines: 0-89586-070-8 or HP1070
Rebuild Big-Block Mopar Engines: 1-55788-190-1 or HP1190
Rebuild Ford V-8 Engines: 0-89586-036-8 or HP1036
Rebuild GenV/Gen VI Big-Block Chevy: 1-55788-357-2 or HP1357
Rebuild Small-Block Chevy Engines: 1-55788-029-8 or HP1029
Rebuild Small-Block Ford Engines: 0-912656-89-1 or HP189
Rebuild Small-Block Mopar Engines: 0-89586-128-3 or HP1128

RESTORATION, MAINTENANCE, REPAIR

Camaro Owner's Handbook ('67–'81): 1-55788-301-7 or HP1301
Camaro Restoration Handbook ('67–'81): 0-89586-375-8 or HP1375
Classic Car Restorer's Handbook: 1-55788-194-4 or HP1194
How to Maintain & Repair Your Jeep: 1-55788-371-8 or HP1371
Mustang Restoration Handbook ('64 1/2–'70): 0-89586-402-9 or HP1402
Tri-Five Chevy Owner's Handbook ('55–'57): 1-55788-285-1 or HP1285

GENERAL REFERENCE

A Fan's Guide to Circle Track Racing: 1-55788-351-3 or HP1351
Auto Math Handbook: 1-55788-020-4 or HP1020
Corvette Tech Q&A: 1-55788-376-9 or HP1376
Ford Total Performance, 1962–1970: 1-55788-327-0 or HP1327
Guide to GM Muscle Cars: 1-55788-003-4 or HP1003

MARINE

Big-Block Chevy Marine Performance: 1-55788-297-5 or HP1297
Small-Block Chevy Marine Performance: 1-55788-317-3 or HP1317

ORDER YOUR COPY TODAY!
All books can be purchased at your favorite retail or online bookstore (use ISBN number), or auto parts store (Use HP part number). You can also order direct from HPBooks by calling toll-free at 800/788-6262, ext. 1.